FRESH

A GREENMARKET COOKBOOK

FRESH
A GREENMARKET COOKBOOK

CAROL E. SCHNEIDER

PANACHE PRESS AT RANDOM HOUSE

Grateful acknowledgment is made to the following photographers for the
use of their work:

Pages 22, 102, 110, 118 copyright © 1989 by Gene Coleman
Pages viii, 18, 30, 40, 56, 94, 106, 114 copyright © 1983, 1985, 1986, 1987,
1988, 1989 by Dick Frank Studios, Inc.
Pages 84, 90 copyright © 1982, 1986 by James Gilmour
Page 52 copyright © 1985 by Leslie Harris
Pages 6, 14, 64, 72 copyright © 1984, 1985, 1986 by Steve Myers
Pages ii, vi, 2, 34, 44, 48, 60, 68, 76, 80, 98, 128, 132 copyright © 1984,
1986, 1987, 1988, 1989 by George Obremski
Pages 26, 136 copyright © 1987, 1988 by Nancy Palubniak
Page 124 copyright © 1985 by Grace Natoli Sheldon
Page 10 copyright © 1987 by Carol Simowitz
Cover photograph and page 144 copyright © 1979 by Michael Skott

Library of Congress Cataloging-in-Publication Data

Schneider, Carol E.
Fresh : a greenmarket cookbook / by Carol E. Schneider.
p. cm.
Includes index.
ISBN 0-679-72602-0
1. Cookery (Fruits) 2. Cookery (Vegetables) I. Title.
TX811.S34 1989   89-3191
641.6′4—dc19

Manufactured in Japan
2 4 6 8 9 7 5 3

Book design by Debbie Glasserman

First Edition

FOR THE MEN AT MY TABLE:
ANDREW, DOUG, ERIC AND JOHN

CONTENTS

I n olden days, to borrow a phrase from Cole Porter, strawberries appeared in June, July brought peaches and raspberries, and you had to wait until August to get a really good tomato. Life had a certain rhythm and pleasure to it; if you cared about food, you could mark the seasons by the array of fruits and vegetables that each one brought. From the first green tips of asparagus and tender pink stalks of rhubarb in the spring to the subdued and somber root vegetables of winter, nature's calendar found eloquent expression in its seasonal bounty.

Modern shipping and agriculture techniques, as well as the expansion of global markets, have made a muddle of the seasons. To be sure, you can still find signs of them at farm stands across the

INTRODUCTION

country. But if you were expected to identify the time of year from a walk through your local greenmarket—or even the produce section of the average supermarket—you might have some trouble.

In some ways, this is a godsend: Having South American raspberries in December, for example, is a real treat, and our menus are undeniably enhanced by the multitude of produce now available year-round. But watch out for the fruits and vegetables that Calvin Trillin has described as "bred by the agribusiness Frankensteins to have a shelf life approximately that of a mop handle." Anyone who goes back a second time for those little cannonballs of peaches and nectarines that show up in February from Chile is probably short on tastebuds. And there is simply no substitute for corn or tomatoes picked fresh from the fields.

Fresh is not so much a celebration of seasons, therefore, as a tribute to fruits and vegetables at their peaks, whenever and wherever these may occur. The book grew out of an annual publication, *The Food Calendar,* which I began to compile over fourteen years ago. During this period of time, our tastes have gravitated toward more natural and healthy ingredients, we have been exposed to a variety of new cuisines, and a dazzling array of new products have graced our markets: from balsamic and raspberry vinegars to yellow watermelons, red pears, and six colors of sweet peppers. As a result, the book has taken on a life of its own. Over sixty new recipes have been developed and tested and I have included a lot more of food lore and history than was offered in the calendars.

Fresh is not an A-to-Z encyclopedia of fruits and vegetables. There is a whole chapter of tomato recipes and only one recipe each for kale and sweet potatoes. Missing entirely are: mangoes and pomegranates, which are simply too much trouble to work with and, I think, better eaten plain; quince, Swiss chard and broccoli rabe, because of my own lack of enthusiasm (it was all I could do to include celery and Brussels sprouts); and some of the more exotic Latin American and Oriental fruits and vegetables that are hard to find in some sections of the country. The recipes are arranged by families of fruits and vegetables, with some major liberties taken at the end of the vegetable section, on the theory that a good cookbook doesn't have to be dull—or predictable.

Fresh foods in their natural state are as pleasing to the eye as they are to the palate, more so, perhaps, than in finished dishes ready for the table. *Fresh,* like *The Food Calendar,* showcases the work of some of this country's most talented food photographers, who have approached their subjects in unaltered states with imagination and an appreciation for their almost abstract beauty. The recipes have also been conceived with color and contrast in mind.

Cooking and entertaining at home seem to be on the upswing after a decade of unprecedented reliance on restaurants and take-out food shops. We are now more sophisticated and busier than our counterparts of ten years ago, and we want to achieve the highest standards of cooking without spending all day in the kitchen. The recipes in *Fresh* have been assembled with these needs in mind—after all, they are my own as well as yours—and I hope you will find that they strike a balance between quality and practicality.

I owe thanks to many people, especially those friends who generously permitted me to use their recipes in this book. Special gratitude must go to my mother, Mary Eitingon, who got me started and has remained my intermittent coach; to Carol Rinzler, for her earliest support and advice; to Geraldine Stutz, for her inspiration and "eye"; to Gilman Park, for his generosity; to Charlotte Mayerson, for her imagination and guidance, even under duress; to Joni Evans, for her encouragement; to David Rosenthal, for my title; to Debbie Glasserman, for her inspired design; and to all the others at Random House for their advice, enthusiasm and good humor, particularly Annik La Farge, Susan Reich and Amy Rhodes. I simply couldn't have finished this book without the help and understanding of my children and John Miller, who were uncomplaining guinea pigs—even for kohlrabi—and for whom I was unavailable too many times during the past eighteen months.

Food purists may argue that fresh foods are best as they come from nature, unhampered by sauces and combinations. And they have a point. But any tomato or zucchini grower knows the mixed blessings of a mountainous harvest, a circle of family and friends never large enough to consume it all, and the prospect of spoilage—or at the very least, boredom—if no attempt at variety is made. The same applies to produce available in markets. Persimmons or rhubarb may only be available even now, for a month or two, but that is time enough to enhance your enjoyment of them by experimenting with a variety of preparations.

A word about ingredients: The most delicious things in life are not necessarily the healthiest, so you'll have to decide whether to use butter or margarine in some of the recipes, or whether to substitute yogurt for sour cream. Where canned or frozen foods work equally well in a recipe, I have noted that fact—but they rarely do. Freshness is the essence of good cooking, and you'll get the best results when you make few or no compromises. On the other hand, why forgo a fresh blueberry-rhubarb pie just because there's no time to make your own crust? It's the fresh fruit that counts. The Basics section at the end of this book offers my own recipes for things like piecrust and pizza dough, chicken stock and fresh tomato sauce, for when you have the time and inclination. If you don't, substitute! Life is too short and cooking is too much fun for cookbooks to be intimidating.

FRESH
A GREENMARKET COOKBOOK

Practically every expert in culinary history—as well as some other busybodies—had a word to say about greens, particularly about the way they were combined in salads. "To make a good salad is to be a brilliant diplomatist..." wrote Oscar Wilde, "to know how much oil one must mix with one's vinegar." Elizabeth Robbins Pennell, in *The Feasts of Autolycus,* thought mixing more important than proportions: "The foolish pour in first their oil, then their vinegar, and leave the rest to chance, with results one shudders to remember." Elizabeth David said "all this talk about 'tossed salads' is a bore" and urged people not to carry on about them.

In fact, salads go way back to the Greeks and Romans, who

GREENS & SPROUTS

already knew the health benefits of eating uncooked vegetables and who concocted what were probably the first salad dressings. Thomas Jefferson grew nineteen varieties of lettuce in his Monticello gardens. In one of the more promising bulletins to come from the food community, a 1980 survey showed that more lettuce was sold in U.S. supermarkets than milk or bread. (Never mind that it was probably iceberg lettuce.)

Today we have a multitude of tasty salad greens available to us: Bibb, Boston, romaine and oakleaf among the many forms of lettuce; sharp chicory and its redheaded cousin, radicchio; peppery watercress; creamy-white Belgian endive; dark green, zesty arugula, and *mâche*, or lamb's lettuce. All should be purchased young, irreproachably fresh and unblemished. Head lettuces should be firm

and heavy, and, when you're ready to use them, all leafy greens should be torn into pieces, not cut, or they will start to go brown.

A few words about some leafy vegetables whose versatility extends beyond the salad bowl: Spinach, which a French proverb calls "the broom of the stomach," is in fact no more mildly laxative than any of the other greens. When you buy it, says Jane Grigson, food expert par excellence, it should "crunch and squeak." Kale, a kind of cabbage-without-a-heart, is fond of cold climates and is said to improve after being touched with frost. Along with collards, mustard greens and its other strongly flavored kin, kale is rich in vitamins and has kept many a farm family alive at the end of winter.

Sprouts, also loaded with minerals and vitamins, especially vitamin C, have now spread from health-food circles into the general diet. If sailors had understood the cause of scurvy, they could have sprouted the beans they carried on board and avoided that killing disease. The earliest edible form of any plant, sprouts are easy to grow at home. (See directions for sprouting wheat berries, for example, on page 7.) The most commonly available sprouts are bean sprouts, known in China three thousand years ago, followed by alfalfa sprouts, whose grown-up version makes good horse and cow feed but poor feed for people. Lentil, wheat-berry and chick-pea sprouts are also good. Choose untreated seeds intended for sprouting rather than those sold for planting, as the latter may have been sprayed with insecticides.

The curly blue-green leaves of kale are especially popular in Scotland and the southern United States. The Scottish poet Robert Burns records a curious Halloween practice: Couples walked hand-in-hand with eyes shut into the fields, where they picked the first kale plant they could find. Its size, shape, and taste were meant to foretell the appearance and temper of their future mates.

CONFETTI SOUP

This soup can also be served chilled, in which case you may have to correct the seasoning.

6 cups Chicken Broth (page 145)
2 onions, chopped
2 cups chopped watercress
1 pound carrots, sliced
2 parsnips, sliced
2 potatoes, peeled and cubed
1 cup heavy cream
1 teaspoon salt
freshly ground pepper to taste

Place stock in large pot. Add vegetables. Cover and cook over moderate heat for 20 minutes, or until vegetables are tender.

Remove from heat and place in blender or food processor, in batches, spinning only until vegetables are broken into small pieces. (Do not let mixture get completely smooth.)

Return to pot and add cream and seasonings. Stir well. Bring to serving temperature.

YIELD: 6 TO 8 SERVINGS

MINESTRONE WITH KALE AND CHICK-PEAS

If you can't find kale, you can substitute cabbage.

1 clove garlic, minced
2 cups chopped onion
1 cup chopped celery
1/4 cup chopped parsley
1/4 cup vegetable oil
3 cups tomato sauce
1 1/4 cups beef broth
1 1-pound, 3-ounce can chick-peas, undrained
1 cup macaroni or spiral noodles
1 small zucchini, thinly sliced
1 cup peas, fresh or frozen
7 cups water
8 cups chopped kale
2 carrots, thinly sliced
1 tablespoon salt
1/4 teaspoon freshly ground black pepper
1/2 teaspoon sage
freshly grated Parmesan cheese

In a large pot sauté garlic, onion, celery and parsley in oil until tender.

Stir in remaining ingredients, except pasta and cheese. Bring to a boil, lower heat and simmer, covered, for 1 hour.

Add macaroni and cook at medium heat for 10 or 15 minutes, until macaroni is tender. Sprinkle with cheese and serve.

YIELD: 8 TO 10 SERVINGS

The so-called spicy sprouts, usually derived from alfalfa and radish, are peppery versions of the do-it-your-self vegetables that require only fresh water, a wide-mouthed con-tainer, room temperature, and a few days' time. Any edible seeds can be sprouted. Certain varieties require some sunlight after germination to turn them green.

This recipe uses two cups of salad, but you can vary the ingredients according to how much you have left over and use whatever greens you have.

2 cups salad, with dressing
1 tablespoon oil
2 cups Chicken Broth (p. 145)

2 cups buttermilk or yogurt
salt and freshly ground pepper to taste
chopped chives or scallions for garnish

Sauté salad briefly in oil. Add chicken broth and cook for 5 minutes only. Remove from heat and allow to cool for about 10 minutes. Place broth mixture in food processor and purée until smooth.

Pour into a bowl, add buttermilk and seasonings and blend well. Chill for 1 hour. Serve garnished with chives.

YIELD: 4 SERVINGS

COMPOSED SALAD WITH NAOMI ROSENBLOOM'S BOURSIN CHEESE DRESSING

This is a particularly attractive way to serve salad when using ingredients of contrasting colors: Each component is arranged separately in sections radiating out from a small dish of dressing in the center. The radicchio and arugula in this salad are assertive enough to balance the strongly flavored dressing.

2 tablespoons wine vinegar
salt and freshly ground pepper to taste
1 tablespoon Dijon mustard
6 tablespoons salad oil
1 clove garlic, crushed
pinch of rosemary

½ package Boursin cheese
1 small head radicchio
1 bunch arugula
1 small head Boston lettuce
1 endive
2 ounces alfalfa sprouts

Combine vinegar, salt, pepper and mustard, stirring well. Slowly add oil, blending thoroughly with a whisk. Add crushed garlic and rosemary and crumble the cheese into the dressing. Refrigerate until serving time.

Wash radicchio, arugula, Boston lettuce and endive and spin dry sepa-rately (or refrigerate in paper towels if you are not serving the salad right away). If sprouts have been grown hydroponically (in water), there is no need to wash them.

When ready to serve, pour salad dressing into a small bowl and place it in the center of a large platter. Arrange the radicchio, sprouts, arugula and Boston lettuce in separate sections around the dressing. You can either make a fifth section with the endive leaves or arrange them individually around the edges of the platter. Use tongs to serve the salad.

YIELD: 4 SERVINGS

JEANNE WESTER NEWMAN'S SPROUTED WHEAT-BERRY BREAD

In order to make this bread, plan to start sprouting the berries three or four days in advance.

Place ¼ cup wheat berries (also called "soft wheat," available in health food stores) in a one-quart Mason jar or similar regular jar and fill with lukewarm water. Place a double thickness of cheesecloth over the mouth and secure with Mason jar ring or a rubber band. Drain water through cheesecloth, fill again, and let soak for two hours. Drain, rinse again and drain. Store jar on its side in a drawer or other dark place. Rinse and drain twice a day for 3 or 4 days, or until 2 cups of sprouts are formed. Place sprouts in a colander, rinse with cold water, drain and store in a plastic bag in refrigerator.

2 packages active dry yeast
3 cups lukewarm water
1 tablespoon salt
¹/₃ cup honey
3 tablespoons oil

3½ cups unbleached flour
2 cups wheat-berry sprouts,
    coarsely chopped
4 cups whole wheat flour

Sprinkle yeast over 1 cup lukewarm water in a large mixing bowl and let sit for 5 minutes. Stir to dissolve yeast. Add remaining water, salt, honey and oil. Mix well.

Stir in unbleached flour and beat dough by hand or with a dough hook in an electric mixer until smooth. Cover and let rise in a warm place until doubled in bulk, about 45 minutes.

Stir in the wheat-berry sprouts and only enough whole wheat flour to make a soft, sticky dough. Turn dough out onto a floured board and knead, with additional flour if necessary, until smooth and elastic, about 10 minutes.

Place in a greased bowl, turning to grease top of dough; cover and let rise in warm place until doubled in bulk, about 1 hour. Grease 2 9- x 5-inch loaf pans. Turn dough onto lightly floured board and knead briefly. Divide in 2,

shape into loaves and place in pans. Cover and let rise again in warm place until doubled in bulk, about 45 minutes.

Preheat oven to 375°F. Bake loaves 25 minutes. Lower oven heat to 300°F., and bake 35 minutes more, or until bottom of loaf sounds hollow when turned out and tapped. Cool on rack.

YIELD: 2 LOAVES

RED LEAF LETTUCE SALAD WITH BALSAMIC VINAIGRETTE

Make more of this salad than you need and then use the leftovers to make the unusual soup on page 5.

1 head red leaf lettuce
1 tablespoon Dijon mustard
2 tablespoons balsamic vinegar
3 tablespoons olive oil

3 tablespoons corn oil
salt and freshly ground pepper
2 scallions, chopped, including
    green part

Wash lettuce and spin dry.

Whisk together mustard and vinegar and gradually add oils, blending well. Season to taste.

Just before serving, tear lettuce leaves into bite-sized pieces, add scallions and toss salad with vinaigrette.

YIELD: 8 SERVINGS

"Prince of vegetables" is the way the Arabs referred to spinach, a member of the goosefoot family that originated in Persia and was introduced into Europe by the Moors around A.D. 1000. Raw spinach is a highly nourishing food—but Popeye and his admirers may have overlooked the fact that its highly touted iron content is virtually lost in cooking and also may be hard for the body to absorb.

PIZZA WITH CREAMED SPINACH AND MUSHROOMS

Because creamed spinach is fairly moist, you'll get better results with this recipe if you prebake the crust.

If you wish, you can mix ordinary button mushrooms with fresh wild mushrooms or reconstituted dried mushrooms to get a more intense flavor. You can also add some crumbled, cooked bacon.

dough for 1 12-inch pizza (p. 147)
2 tablespoons butter or margarine
12 ounces fresh mushrooms, sliced

1 cup Creamed Spinach (see preceding recipe)
1/2 pound mozzarella cheese, grated
2 ounces Parmesan cheese, grated

Prepare dough according to recipe on page 147 and let rise.

In a large frying pan, heat butter and sauté mushrooms until they begin to yield up moisture. Drain and set aside.

When dough has risen, preheat oven to 450°F., roll out dough and place in pan according to recipe. Prick the crust in several places and bake for 10 minutes. Remove from pan.

Spread creamed spinach on surface of crust and top with mushrooms. Sprinkle with cheeses.

Bake for about 15 minutes more, or until crust and cheeses are golden brown.

YIELD: 4 SERVINGS (2 SLICES APIECE)

CREAMED SPINACH

If possible, buy your spinach loose, rather than in bags, so you can avoid damaged leaves and those with thick, woody stems. And take the extra time to rinse the leaves twice, since there is nothing worse than gritty spinach.

2 1/2 pounds fresh spinach
1 tablespoon butter or margarine
1 tablespoon flour
3/4 cup sour cream

1/2 teaspoon salt or to taste
1/4 teaspoon nutmeg
freshly ground pepper to taste

Remove larger stems and any roots from spinach leaves and place leaves in a sinkful of lukewarm water. Let soak for a few minutes, then remove leaves, drain out water, clean sink and fill again. Dunk the leaves until they are completely free of dirt, then drain.

Cook the spinach in a very small amount of boiling salted water, covered, until tender. Drain thoroughly and chop well or put through a food mill.

Melt butter and stir in the flour. Add sour cream and cook, stirring, until mixture thickens. Add the spinach and cook until heated through. Add salt, nutmeg and pepper.

YIELD: 4 SERVINGS

PITA ROLL-UPS WITH LILLY'S GREEN SAUCE

This is a great trick to get a crowd to cook its own meal. It also gives you a clever way to clean out your refrigerator. Make the sauce, provide the pita bread and bowls of this and that. Vary the quantities of bread and fillings according to how many you have to feed. The oversized pitas are available in stores that specialize in Middle Eastern foods.

Lilly's Green Sauce

small bunch of parsley
small bunch of dill
4 scallions, trimmed including
   green part
1 clove garlic, sliced
1 tablespoon Dijon mustard

$1/2$ cup corn oil
$1/4$ cup wine or tarragon
   vinegar
$1/2$ cup yogurt
$1/2$ cup Mayonnaise (page 145)
salt and freshly ground pepper
   to taste

Fillings

Small bowls of any or all of the following or whatever other tidbits you want to recycle:

shredded lettuce, watercress
  sprouts
chopped tomatoes, peppers,
   avocados, cucumbers
cooked bacon slices or bits
strips of ham, turkey,
   leftover chicken

coarsely grated cheeses—Swiss,
   Cheddar, mozzarella, Parmesan
grated carrots
sliced fresh mushrooms
1 package of 8 individual large
   (8-to-9-inch) pita breads
squares of aluminum foil

Early in the day, make the green sauce: Place parsley, dill, scallions and garlic in food processor and spin until minced. Add remaining ingredients and process until smooth. Correct seasoning and chill.

When ready to assemble, prepare bowls of fillings. Just before serving, preheat oven to 400°F. Run a small, sharp knife around the circumference of each pita, separating it carefully into 2 halves. (If you do this too early, they will dry out.) Invite guests to spread the inside of each half with green sauce, add desired fillings at one end, and roll up. To secure, place each roll diagonally on an aluminum foil square and roll up inside foil, tucking in ends. Place in oven for 10 minutes until cheese melts. Serve immediately.

JULIE SPITZER'S SPINACH LASAGNA

9 lasagna strips
2 cups coarsely chopped
   cooked spinach
2 pounds small-curd cottage
   cheese
2 eggs
2 cloves garlic, peeled
   and crushed

salt and freshly ground pepper
   to taste
handful of parsley, chopped
1 pound Monterey Jack cheese,
   coarsely grated
1 cup coarsely grated Parmesan
   cheese
additional grated Parmesan for
   topping

Preheat oven to 350°F.

Cook lasagna according to package directions and drain. Run pasta under cold water, drain again and lay flat in a single layer on paper towels until needed.

Drain spinach well and squeeze in a fabric dish towel to remove all moisture. Set aside.

Combine cottage cheese, eggs, garlic, seasonings and parsley, and mix well until blended.

In a well greased 9- x 13-inch baking pan, place a layer of noodles. Spread half the cottage cheese mixture on top, followed by half the spinach and half the grated cheeses. Repeat layers, ending with a layer of lasagna. Sprinkle with additional Parmesan and bake for 45 minutes.

YIELD: 6 SERVINGS

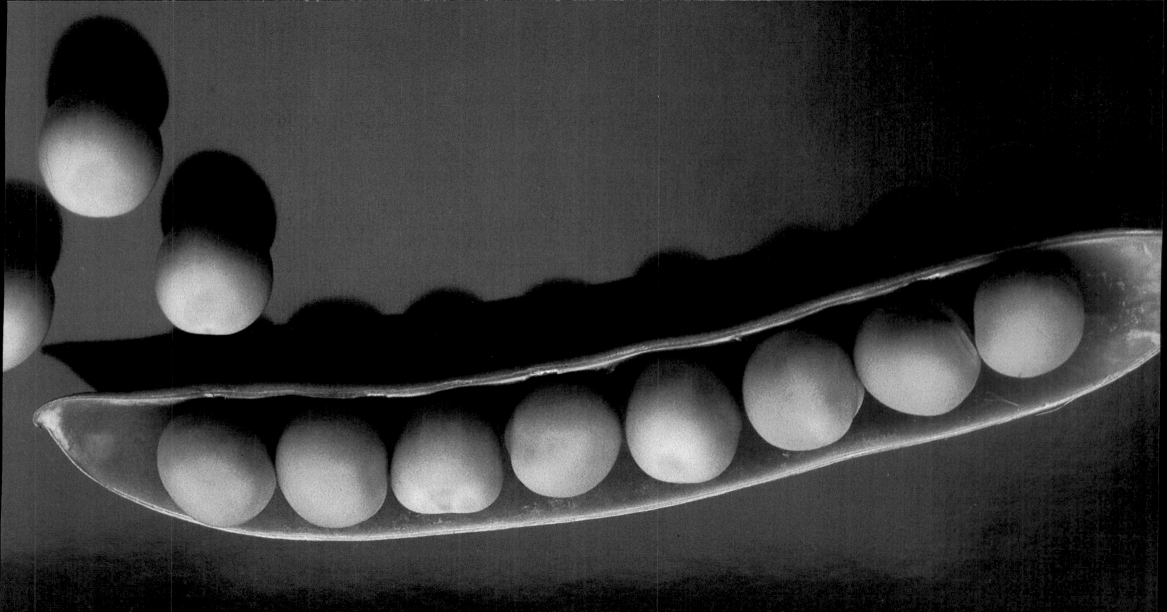

People who scorn peas and beans as "poor man's meat" are missing both the point and the pleasure of these most ancient of vegetables, the legumes. They have many virtues: They can be dried and stored for future use; they have a high nutritional and caloric value, especially in their dried state; they come in a rainbow of colors and shapes; they have recently been shown to lower cholesterol; and they are a bargain, to boot.

The oldest pea we know of has been carbon dated by archaeologists at 9750 B.C., from the border between Burma and Thailand. The earliest varieties were field peas, grown to be dried and saved for winter. Sweet green garden peas reached a peak of popularity in seventeenth-century France. Madame de Maintenon described

PEAS & BEANS

them as "a fad, a fury" in the court of Louis XIV, whose physician reported the Sun King laid low by his overindulgence. Some say the word "pea" comes from the Sanskrit *pis*, to divide, suggesting the peas as portions of the pod. Others point to the Latin name for this vegetable, *pisum*, which became *pise* in old English. As our language evolved, the "s" sound was thought to be a plural, which paved the way for the totally incorrect singular form, "pea."

A wrinkled pea is a better pea, say food experts, despite the American obsession with beauty and size. As peas mature, they gain starch and lose sugar, so the smooth large pea of our ideal and Birds Eye's pride is actually less sweet and succulent than the younger imperfectly formed one. When buying fresh peas, look for bright green pods that are slightly velvety and well filled without being swollen. (A pound of peas in the pod equals about one cup shelled.) And don't overlook snow peas and the newer sugar snap peas, whose crisp and juicy edible pods offer instant gratification.

Beans, also grown since prehistoric times, enjoy a particularly rich place in folklore and history. The Romans ended funerals with beanfests and thought them unlucky, yet used beans as counters in their voting. Scottish witches were said to ride on beanstalks, ghosts could be banished by spitting beans at them, and roasted beans were buried to stave off toothache and smallpox. Texans, contradicting the Romans, still serve beans (black-eyed peas, actually) on New Year's Day for good luck.

Although found in a bewildering array of varieties, beans can basically be broken down into two market categories: snap or pod beans, eaten shell and all while still unripe, such as green or string beans and wax beans; and shell beans, whose fruit we remove from the pod when they are fully mature. Into this latter category fall lima, kidney and soy beans; the oversized pods of fava or broad beans with their furry white interiors; and cranberry beans with their attractive rosy streaks, among others. The word "haricot," a family encompassing virtually every category above except broad beans and soybeans, is more commonly heard in France these days than here, but is actually a corruption of the Aztec *ayacotl*, indicating its New World origins.

The "string bean" is a misnomer in this day of sophisticated cultivation, since the strings have been virtually eliminated from green beans by popular demand. All beans should be crisp and brightly colored, without scars or discoloration, and pod beans should break easily with a snap, hence their alternate name.

When Esau renounced his birth-right for a dish of lentils, he showed wisdom in the ways of food, if nothing else: These small, flat, leguminous seeds, with colors ranging from brown to red to green, share top nutritional and economic value with their kin among the peas and beans, and have an even higher protein content.

MAIN-COURSE LENTIL SOUP

Vinegar? Yes. Unlikely though it sounds, a good splash of vinegar adds an unusual sparkle to this down-home soup. Add it just before serving so the bite survives.

1 pound lentils	2 large carrots, peeled and sliced
2 stalks celery, chopped	1 bay leaf
2 medium tomatoes, peeled, seeded and chopped	2 teaspoons salt
1 pound kielbasa or other smoked sausage	freshly ground pepper to taste
8 cups Chicken Broth (page 145)	2 teaspoons cider vinegar
1 large onion, chopped	
2 cloves garlic, minced	

Wash lentils under cold running water and drain. Place in a large stock pot with whole kielbasa and all other ingredients except vinegar. Bring to a boil and simmer, covered, for 1 hour, or until lentils are soft. Remove sausage and bay leaf from soup and set aside.

Strain soup into a large pot. Remove 4 cups of the solids from the strainer and spin them briefly in a blender or purée in 2 batches in a food processor. Stir into liquid and add remaining solids.

Cut sausage into ¼-inch slices and return to soup. Add vinegar, correct seasonings and heat the soup to serving temperature.

YIELD: 8 SERVINGS

CHILLED GREEN BEAN AND ARTICHOKE SOUP

½ pound fresh green beans	2 cups milk
1 8-ounce can artichoke hearts, packed in water	salt and freshly ground pepper to taste
1 large onion, chopped	chopped watercress for garnish
½ cup olive oil	chopped parsley for garnish

Trim ends of beans. In a small amount of boiling water, simmer them until just tender, then drain.

Drain artichoke hearts, reserving liquid from can.

Sauté onion in olive oil until transparent and combine (including oil) with beans and artichokes in the blender. Purée until smooth, adding a little of the reserved artichoke liquid if mixture is too thick to blend easily. Chill.

Just before serving, add milk and season to taste with salt and pepper. Mix thoroughly. Garnish with watercress and parsley.

YIELD: 8 SERVINGS

CURRIED BEEF WITH PEAS, RAISINS AND ALMONDS

This is a perfect recipe for a busy day—it takes only about twenty minutes to make.

2 tablespoons butter or margarine
2 large onions, diced
1 clove garlic, minced
1 pound lean ground chuck
1 tablespoon flour
1 tablespoon curry powder or to taste
1 teaspoon ground ginger

2 tablespoons raisins
1/4 cup chopped blanched almonds
1 1/4 cups beef broth
1 cup peas
salt and freshly ground pepper to taste
rice

Melt butter in a large skillet and sauté onions and garlic until they begin to turn golden.

Add meat and cook, breaking up with a fork, until it loses its pink color. Stir in flour, curry powder and ginger and cook for a minute or 2.

Add raisins, almonds and broth. Bring to a boil and simmer, covered, for 10 minutes. Add peas and simmer for 5 minutes more. Season to taste and serve over hot rice.

YIELD: 4 TO 5 SERVINGS

SEAFOOD STIR-FRY WITH SNOW PEAS

2 teaspoons cornstarch
2 tablespoons water
3 tablespoons soy sauce
2 tablespoons dry sherry
4 tablespoons peanut oil
1 medium onion, minced
2 cloves garlic, minced

2 teaspoons minced fresh ginger
1 pound bay scallops, rinsed and drained on paper towels
1 pound fresh medium shrimp, peeled and deveined
1/2 pound snow peas, strings removed

In a small bowl, mix cornstarch, cold water, soy sauce and sherry. Set aside.

Heat 2 tablespoons of the oil in a wok or large frying pan. Add onion, garlic and ginger and cook only until onion is transparent. Add remaining 2 tablespoons oil, heat and add scallops and shrimp. Stir-fry over fairly high heat 3 to 4 minutes, then add snow peas and continue cooking until shrimp turns pink.

Add cornstarch mixture and bring to a boil. Cook a minute or 2 more. Serve immediately over rice.

YIELD: 4 SERVINGS

BEEF STEW WITH LIMA BEANS, CARROTS AND PARSNIPS

If you can't find fresh lima beans, the frozen ones make a perfectly acceptable substitute in this recipe.

1/2 cup flour
salt and freshly ground pepper to
    taste
2 1/2 pounds lean stewing beef, cut
    in cubes
3 to 4 tablespoons butter or
    margarine
1 large onion, roughly chopped
1 large clove garlic, minced
1 cup beef broth
1/2 cup red wine

3 tablespoons tomato paste
1 teaspoon mixed pickling spices
1 bay leaf
3 carrots, pared and cut into
    chunks
3 parsnips, pared and cut into
    chunks
1 1/2 pounds fresh lima beans
    shelled, or 1 10-ounce package
    frozen limas

Mix flour, salt and pepper in a plastic bag and toss meat lightly to dredge, several pieces at a time. Shake off excess.

In a large heavy casserole or frying pan, heat 1 tablespoon of the butter until it sizzles and sauté about half the beef cubes until brown on all sides. Chunks of meat should not touch one another or they will steam instead of browning. Repeat, adding butter as necessary, until all the meat is browned. Remove from pan and set aside.

Add a little more butter to the same pan, if necessary, and sauté onion and garlic until they are lightly browned. Pour in broth and wine and heat over low flame, stirring to loosen all browned bits on bottom of pan.

Add tomato paste and stir to blend. Place pickling spices in a tea ball or cheesecloth pouch, then add it and bay leaf to sauce. Return meat to pan. Cover pan and bring to a boil; reduce heat and simmer for 1 hour, or until meat is tender.

Add carrots and simmer for 10 minutes. Add parsnips and lima beans and simmer for 20 minutes more.

YIELD: 6 TO 8 SERVINGS

PEA SALAD WITH DILL

If you are worrying about the heavy dose of cholesterol in this recipe, you can substitute low-fat yogurt for the sour cream. But it won't be as good.

3 cups fresh green peas, shelled
1 cup sour cream
1/3 cup Mayonnaise (pages 145–
    46)

1/4 cup chopped scallions,
    including green part
1/4 cup freshly snipped dill
salt and freshly ground pepper to
    taste

Place peas in small amount of boiling water, cover and simmer until just tender (time will vary with size of peas). Drain and let cool.

Mix together the remaining ingredients, season to taste, and toss with the cooled peas. Chill. Serve on a bed of spring greens.

YIELD: 8 SERVINGS

The Romans used beans as a method of counting the votes at election time, and even today account-ants are sometimes called "bean counters." A Latin proverb "abstineto a fabis" warned men to stay away from beans—meaning, no doubt, not to meddle in politics—but who could resist when the beans in question are the glorious, color-fully striated cranberry beans?

CRANBERRY BEANS IN TOMATO SAUCE

Don't expect these beans to maintain their vivid color after cooking.

3 pounds fresh cranberry beans, shelled (about 4 cups)	1½ cups Fresh Tomato Sauce (page 146)
1 cup loosely packed, cubed bacon	½ teaspoon salt
2 medium onions, thinly sliced	freshly ground pepper to taste
2 cloves garlic, minced	1 teaspoon dried sage
	½ teaspoon dried basil

Cook beans in boiling salted water until tender, about 30 minutes.

In the meantime, sauté bacon cubes in a large frying pan until fat is rendered. Add onions and garlic and cook over low heat until soft and light brown. Add the tomato sauce, seasonings and herbs, and simmer for 5 minutes.

When they are ready, drain beans and add to frying pan. Cover and simmer over low heat for 15 minutes so flavors can blend.

YIELD: 8 SERVINGS

PEAS WITH PROSCIUTTO

3 cups fresh green peas, shelled	1 tablespoon chopped fresh parsley
1 small onion, finely chopped	½ teaspoon salt
2 tablespoons butter or margarine	freshly ground pepper to taste
¾ cup chopped prosciutto	6 tablespoons freshly grated Parmesan cheese
1 tablespoon minced fresh basil	

Cook peas in a small amount of boiling water just until tender. Drain.

Meanwhile, sauté onion in butter until wilted. Add prosciutto, herbs, salt and pepper, and cook over low flame. Add peas and cook for 1 minute. Just before serving, stir in Parmesan cheese.

YIELD: 6 SERVINGS

WAX BEANS WITH WATERCRESS AND PINE NUTS

Sometimes wax beans seem appropriately named—in the taste department, anyway. In this recipe the sharp taste of the greens and the crunch of the pine nuts are a perfect foil for the plain taste of the beans.

1 pound wax beans
6 sprigs watercress
6 sprigs parsley
2 tablespoons butter or margarine

2 tablespoons pine nuts
1 clove garlic, crushed
salt and freshly ground pepper to taste

Pinch the ends off the wax beans, rinse and drain, and steam over boiling water for about 12 minutes, or until just tender.

In the meantime, remove watercress and parsley stems and chop the leaves. Melt butter and add pine nuts, garlic and chopped herbs.

When beans are done, drain and toss with butter mixture. Season to taste with salt and pepper.

YIELD: 6 SERVINGS

PASTA CON PISELLI

3 tablespoons butter or margarine
1 cup heavy cream
1/2 teaspoon salt
1/4 teaspoon white pepper
pinch of nutmeg

2 pounds fresh peas, shelled (about 2 cups)
1/2 pound pasta (sea shells, spirals, et cetera)
1 cup freshly grated Parmesan cheese

Melt butter with 2/3 cup of the cream in saucepan. Simmer, stirring often, about 20 minutes or until mixture thickens. Stir in seasonings and set aside.

Cook peas in a small amount of boiling water until just tender, about 2 to 4 minutes. Drain and set aside.

In a separate pan, cook pasta according to package directions until just tender. Drain and combine with peas. Return to pan and add sauce, remaining cream, and cheese and heat over low flame, stirring gently until combined.

YIELD: 6 SERVINGS AS A SIDE DISH

It's hard to imagine anyone mistrusting a tomato in the sixteenth century—especially since there was nary a chance of finding the tough, invulnerable rock of today's cellophane wrapped cartons. Tomatoes, however, had a long and hard road to popular acceptance. Of Mexican or South American origin, they were introduced into Europe in the late 1500s and were immediately viewed with suspicion and distaste. An Italian herbalist listed them among the dangerous and even poisonous narcotic herbs; they were rumored to be aphrodisiac, and nicknamed "love apples"; and used solely as decorative plants for several centuries.

What accounts for this wrongheadedness? Food historian Waverley Root wonders if the perpetrator of this myth might not have eaten

TOMATOES

the wrong part of the plant, the leaves, which indeed have been found to be toxic. Whatever the cause, it took hundreds of years for anyone to dare eat a tomato raw, and two nineteenth-century cookbooks actually advised cooking them for no less than three hours, which would surely purge them of their venom. But wrongheadedness can work both ways: André Simon, in his 1938 *Concise Encyclopedia of Gastronomy*—perhaps overly enthusiastic about our century's newly discovered joy in eating tomatoes raw—wrote, "A cooked tomato is like a cooked oyster: ruined."

Botanically, the tomato is classified as a fruit, yet a Supreme Court ruling in 1893 established that it be called a vegetable for the purposes of trade since it was used as such. American markets generally offer four types: the garden variety, the larger beefsteak tomato, the small round cherry tomato (which was probably the original of the breed), and the plum or pear tomato.

The best ripe tomatoes have a rich red or yellow color, a slight softness, and are well formed and free of blemishes or "sunburn," the green or yellow areas near the stem scar. You can partially ripen pink-to-light-red tomatoes from the garden on a sunny windowsill or in an open, warm place, but you simply won't get the full flavor or color of the vine-ripened fruit. In fact, it's better to take a malformed but fully ripe tomato fresh from the earth—with its unmistakable scent—than the most perfect-looking pretender from the supermarket shelf. For this reason, many people only use fresh tomatoes two or three months of the year.

COLD TOMATO-DILL SOUP

This recipe is delicious when made with fresh, ripe tomatoes, but if they are not at their peak, you can substitute 3 cups of tomato juice for the tomatoes and water.

3 large or 4 medium tomatoes
1 teaspoon salt
freshly ground pepper to taste
2 tablespoons tomato paste
1/4 cup water
4 scallions, minced, including green part

pinch of thyme
grated rind of 1/2 lemon
3 to 4 tablespoons freshly snipped dill
sugar
1 cup sour cream

Peel tomatoes by dunking them in boiling water for 20 seconds; the skin will then come off easily. Slice and place in saucepan with salt, pepper, tomato paste and water. Cover and simmer for 15 minutes.

Cool and purée in blender.

Remove from blender. Add scallions, thyme, lemon rind, dill and a pinch of sugar to taste. Chill. Just before serving, blend in sour cream.

YIELD: 4 TO 6 SERVINGS

JASON EPSTEIN'S BRUSCHETTA WITH TOMATOES AND SQUID

Bruschetta is the Italian version of garlic bread—toasted Italian bread rubbed with cut garlic and drizzled with a good olive oil. This version adds an earthy tomato and squid topping.

2 plum tomatoes
6 ounces small squid
2 tablespoons extra-virgin olive oil
1 large clove garlic, minced
salt and freshly ground pepper to taste
1 large clove garlic, cut diagonally

hot pepper flakes
splash of lemon juice
1 tablespoon chopped flat-leaf parsley
6 slices good quality Italian bread, cut diagonally
taste

Trim ends of tomatoes and cut in half lengthwise. Squeeze out seeds and juice end chop. Set aside in a small bowl.

Clean squid and dry well with paper towels. With a sharp knife, cut bodies and tentacles into small pieces. In a small frying pan, heat olive oil until very hot. Add minced garlic and squid and sear quickly, stirring frequently, just until flesh turns opaque. Sprinkle with salt, pepper and hot pepper flakes to taste. Remove from heat and drain, reserving oil. Add squid to tomatoes in bowl. Add lemon juice and parsley and toss well.

Toast the slices of bread lightly. While still hot rub each slice with a piece of cut garlic and brush with reserved squid-flavored oil. Top with tomato and squid mixture.

YIELD: 6 SERVINGS AS AN ANTIPASTO

TOMATOES STUFFED WITH LITTLE GOAT CHEESE SOUFFLÉS

From Jane Grigson's The Mushroom Feast, *on the tomato: "A number of rare or newly experienced foods have been claimed to be aphrodisiacs. At one time this quality was even ascribed to the tomato. Reflect on this when you are next preparing the family salad."*

6 large or 8 medium tomatoes
1 cup of milk
pinch of cayenne
pinch of nutmeg
2 tablespoons butter or margarine

2 tablespoons flour
3 eggs, separated
salt and white pepper to taste
3 tablespoons crumbled goat
   cheese
2 teaspoons chopped chives

Preheat oven to 350°F.

Cut a thin slice from stem end of each tomato and scoop out pulp, taking care not to pierce the shells. Reserve pulp for another use. Turn tomatoes upside down on paper towels to drain.

Scald milk with cayenne and nutmeg. Remove from heat and reserve.

In another saucepan, melt butter, stir in flour and cook, whisking for 1 minute. Add milk, bring to a boil, and simmer, continuing to whisk, for 2 minutes or until thick and smooth. Remove from heat and beat in the egg yolks, one at a time. Add salt and pepper. Stir in goat cheese. Check seasonings, then cover and cool slightly.

Beat egg whites until they form stiff peaks and fold lightly into cheese mixture.

Sprinkle insides of tomatoes with salt and 1 teaspoon of the chives. Place in a baking dish just large enough to hold them closely. Fill each tomato with cheese mixture.

Bake 20 minutes or until soufflés are puffed and slightly brown. Sprinkle with remaining chives and serve immediately.

YIELD: 6 TO 8 SERVINGS AS A SIDE DISH OR APPETIZER

CHERRY TOMATOES TWO WAYS

Use a pint of tomatoes for each of these recipes but *don't* use the very tiny yellow cherry tomatoes for the first recipe. It would take a saint to stuff them.

Stuffed

1 pint cherry tomatoes
5 ounces Boursin cheese

3/4 cup sour cream
2 scallions, chopped, including
   green part

Cut a thin slice off the top of each tomato and scoop out the pulp with a baby spoon or serrated grapefruit spoon. (You can reserve the pulp for another use.)

Combine cheese, sour cream and scallions, and stuff each tomato with the mixture. Chill before serving.

Marinated

1 pint cherry tomatoes
1/2 cup freshly squeezed lemon
   juice
1/4 cup snipped basil leaves

3/4 cup good olive oil
salt and freshly pepper to
   taste

Prick each tomato all over with a toothpick.

Mix lemon juice and basil. Pour oil over mixture, whisking until liquids are thoroughly blended. Season to taste.

Place tomatoes in a shallow glass dish and cover with lemon-oil dressing. Chill for several hours, tossing occasionally.

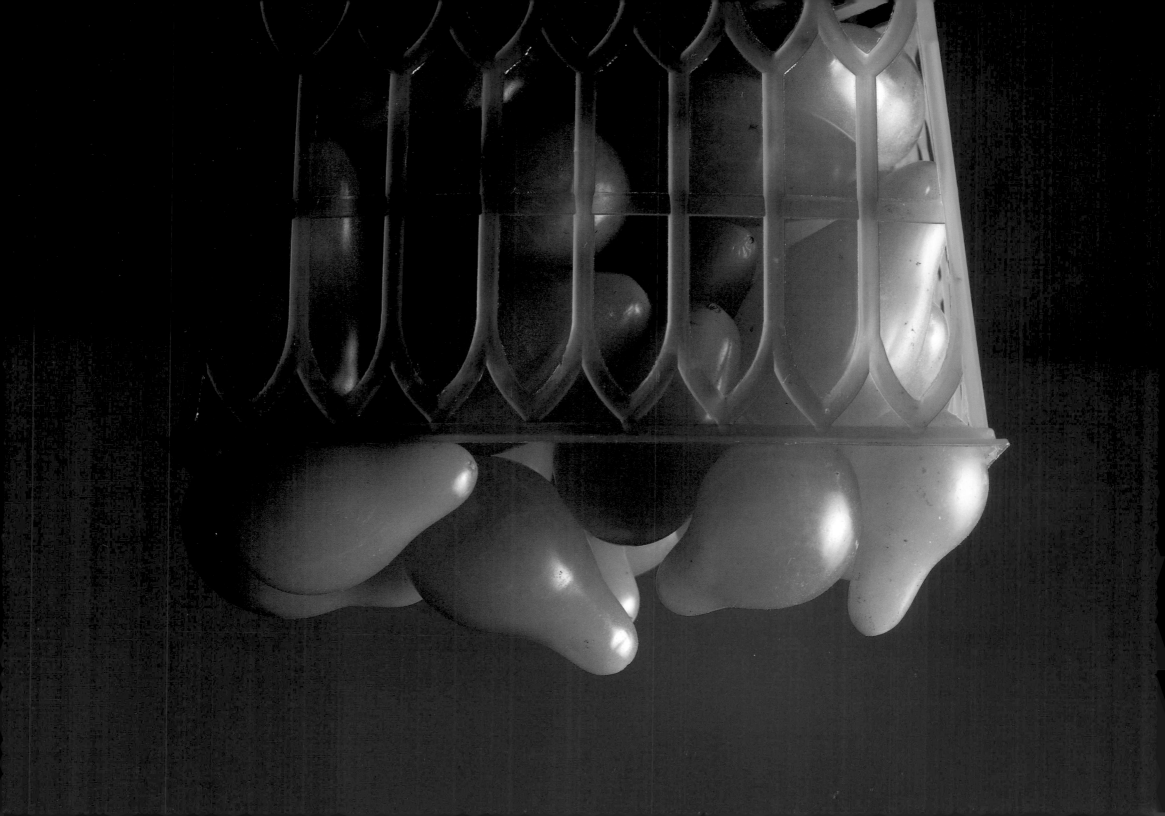

While the yellow tomato might appear to be the work of latter-day botanical wizards (like the yellow pepper and the yellow watermelon), it was in fact the first variety of tomato known to man. The original Peruvian tomato was small in size and was called pomo d'oro *or* pomodoro *(literally, golden apple), by the Italians who borrowed it and bred it in the sixteenth century.*

YELLOW TOMATO, CHEESE AND ONION PIE

Red tomatoes will, of course, work just fine in this recipe. But this is a pretty way to use the large golden ones.

1 10 inch deep-dish unbaked pie shell made with Basic Pie Pastry (page 148)
3 tablespoons butter or margarine
2 large onions, sliced (about 4 cups)
1/2 pound Gruyère cheese
2 tablespoons flour

3/4 pound yellow tomatoes (one large beefsteak tomato is perfect)
1 1/2 tablespoons fresh thyme (or 1 1/2 teaspoons dried)
2 eggs
3/4 cup heavy cream

Line pie dish with pastry and chill.

In a large frying pan, melt butter and sauté onions over medium heat until they turn golden, which will take about 30 minutes. Stir frequently.

Preheat oven to 350°F.

Grate the cheese and toss with the flour. Set aside.

When onions are done, assemble the pie: Sprinkle an ample handful of cheese mixture on pie crust. Spread onions on top. Slice the tomato and arrange slices over the onions. Sprinkle with thyme and the remaining cheese.

Beat eggs with cream and pour over pie. Bake for 35 to 40 minutes, or until top is golden brown and pie is firm in the middle.

YIELD: 6 SERVINGS

TOMATO-BASIL STUFFING FOR FISH

This stuffing is delicious with striped bass or bluefish, but you can use it for any fish that has been cleaned and split.

4 medium-sized, ripe tomatoes, sliced
2 large onions, thickly sliced
1/2 cup chopped fresh basil

1/2 cup finely chopped fresh parsley
1/2 teaspoon finely chopped garlic
1 teaspoon salt
freshly ground pepper to taste

Combine all ingredients in a bowl and toss slightly.

Use stuffing to loosely fill a 6-pound fish or 2 3-pounders. Fasten sides of fish with skewers and grill or bake.

Cherry tomatoes are best for eating as a snack or salad ingredient, despite their predilection for flying out of your mouth or squirting your neighbor. To avoid this, simply cut them in half. They have too little pulp relative to their skin to make a good sauce, but they make a lovely and colorful garnish to a hot meal if you sauté them lightly in butter.

OKRA WITH TOMATOES AND PEPPERS

Some people think okra is too "slimy," but if you take care not to cut into the pod when you're cleaning it you'll avoid releasing the gummy substance.

1 pound fresh okra
4 tablespoons ($1/2$ stick) butter or margarine
2 teaspoons minced fresh ginger
1 large red pepper, chopped
1 large green pepper, chopped
2 cloves garlic, minced
1 large onion, chopped
3 large tomatoes, cored and sliced
$1/2$ teaspoon salt
freshly ground pepper to taste

Wash okra, dry well and trim caps without cutting into pods. Steam over 1 inch of boiling water for 6 to 8 minutes, or until just tender. Drain well and set aside.

In a large frying pan, melt butter and sauté onion, garlic, peppers and ginger for 3 to 4 minutes. Add tomato slices, cover and simmer for 10 minutes. Add okra, salt and pepper, and simmer more for 2 minutes, until okra is hot.

YIELD: 6 SERVINGS

CHERRY TOMATOES WITH SHALLOTS AND PARSLEY

Whether you use red or yellow cherry tomatoes or a combination of both, this makes a colorful side dish.

2 tablespoons butter or margarine
$1/4$ cup freshly snipped parsley
$1/4$ cup chopped shallots
1 pint cherry tomatoes, halved
Salt and freshly ground pepper to taste

In a large frying pan, melt butter and sauté shallots for a few minutes, until wilted. Add tomatoes and sauté for a few minutes more, until just heated through.

Toss with salt and pepper, sprinkle with parsley and serve immediately.

YIELD: 4 SERVINGS

TABBOULEH

Bulgur, or cracked wheat, is available in most specialty and health food stores as well as in many supermarkets. There is no acceptable substitute for either this or the fresh mint in this Middle Eastern salad. No cooking is required, but the wheat needs to steep for about an hour and also needs time to chill.

1 cup medium bulgur wheat
4 cups boiling water
1 cup minced parsley
1/2 cup minced fresh mint
1/2 cup scallions, minced, including green part

2 medium tomatoes, diced (about 1 1/2 cups)
1/2 cup fresh lemon juice
1/2 cup olive oil
1 teaspoon salt
freshly ground pepper to taste

Place wheat in a mixing bowl and steep, covered, in the boiling water for 1 hour, or until wheat is light and fluffy. Drain off any excess water and shake the wheat in a strainer until it is very dry. Add the remaining ingredients to the wheat and mix thoroughly. Chill at least 1 hour.

YIELD: 6 to 8 SERVINGS

COLD ZUCCHINI-STUFFED TOMATOES

Don't throw away your leftover rice—transform it into this summer offering.

6 medium-sized, firm ripe tomatoes
3 tablespoons olive oil
3 large cloves garlic, minced
3 cups grated, unpeeled zucchini
2 tablespoons chopped fresh or 1 1/2 teaspoons dried basil

salt and feshly ground pepper to taste
3/4 cup cooked rice
2 tablespoons coarsely grated lemon peel
Mayonnaise (pages 145–46)

Cut 1/2" slice from stem end of each tomato and scoop out the pulp, leaving shells intact. Dice 1 1/2 cups of the tomato pulp.

In hot oil, sauté garlic, zucchini and pulp for several minutes. Add seasonings and cook, uncovered, until most of the juices have evaporated.

Stir in rice and lemon peel. Fill tomatoes with this mixture. Chill. Just before serving, cover with a layer of mayonnaise, and garnish with additional basil.

YIELD: 6 SERVINGS

Given the importance of tomatoes in Italian, French and Spanish cooking, it is amazing to learn that they weren't known in Europe until the 16th century, and even then were regarded with suspicion. They were sometimes dubbed "apples of Peru," indicating a Peruvian origin, and their English name derives from the Aztec tomatl, or "swelling fruit."

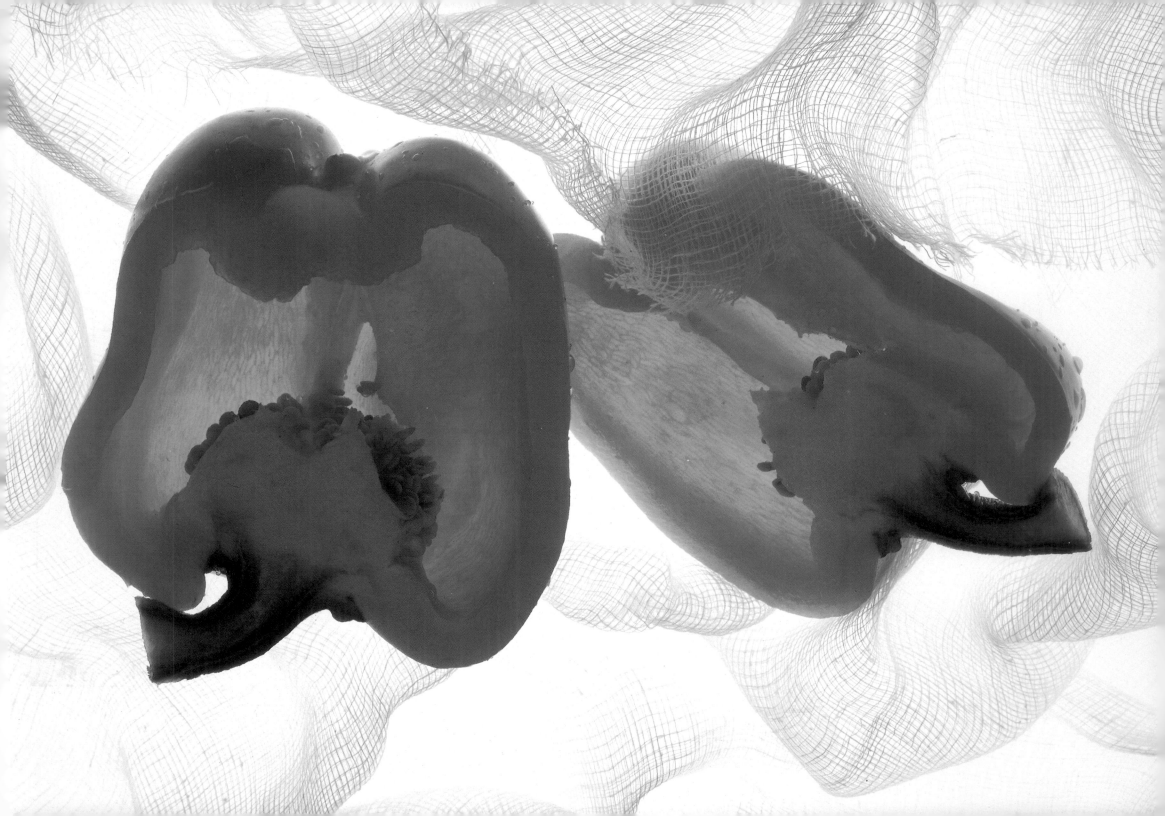

When is a pepper not a pepper? When it's a capsicum, the true name for the vegetable we know today as the sweet or hot pepper. The mistake dates back to Columbus: When New World Indians served him a hot spice on his food, he mistook it for the black pepper derived from peppercorns, and named it accordingly. It was actually chili, from the "hot" branch of the capsicums. But the die was cast.

These peppers, or capsicums, were introduced in Europe after the voyages of Columbus, who opened up a whole new world of food with his travels in America. The American pepper comes in two major types: the large "sweet" or bell pepper, and the smaller chili. A good rule of thumb is that the larger the pepper, the milder it will

PEPPERS & EGGPLANTS

be—though given the great many varieties of this plant, look before you leap. As to color, generally speaking red peppers are the fully ripe form of the green. Pimentos and paprika come from the mild red pepper. Tabasco sauce, chili and cayenne are products of the hotter chilies. The word "capsicum" may come from the latin *capsa*, or box (referring to its boxlike enclosure for its seeds), or from the Greek *capto*, meaning "I bite," which suggests the more fiery varieties.

Today's market offers us a kaleidescope of peppers, in colors ranging from almost white to deep green, and from the yellow-orange hues into the reds and purples. Look for those with a strong color, a glossy sheen, and firm, not flimsy walls (though the yellow-through-red varieties are generally softer than the others).

The eggplant comes from a totally different corner of the world: tropical Asia, probably India. It was no better received than the tomato when it was introduced in England in the sixteenth century; the Brits called it "mad apple" because they believed it caused insanity. John Gerard attributed it with a "mischievous qualitie" in his 1597 *Herball* and warned prudent Englishman off this perilous vegetable. Happily, cooks in other parts of the world knew better, to which we owe the wide variety of eggplant recipes available today. They come from all parts of the world…the Mediterranean, Russia, Japan.

Americans are most familiar with the dark purple variety, but rarer forms can be green, yellow, ash colored or white. The latter color, together with its egglike swell, probably inspired its English name, and white eggplants are increasingly available in markets today. The also come in several shapes and sizes. Italians often use very small eggplants. The Japanese use a long thin version in many recipes. Whatever the color or shape, select firm, shiny eggplants that are heavy for their size with bright green caps and no scars or cuts. Eggplant flesh is spongy and tends to absorb a great deal of oil during cooking. This can be avoided by salting and draining the slices before you sauté them.

When Peter Piper picked a peck of pickled peppers, he could have chosen from among a huge variety cultivated all over the world and originally from Central America. A pound of peppers, trimmed and chopped, will yield about four cups. As to a peck of pickled peppers—that's eight quarts. Eight pounds, if anyone cares.

MARINATED EGGPLANT CUBES WITH FRESH HERBS

Serve these with toothpicks as an hors d'oeuvre, or with triangles of toast or black bread spread with cream cheese as a first course. If you cannot find the particular fresh herbs mentioned below, feel free to substitute others: basil, oregano, tarragon, et cetera.

1 1-pound eggplant, unpeeled	1 teaspoon chopped fresh marjoram
1/4 cup virgin olive oil	1 teaspoon chopped fresh thyme
2 tablespoons balsamic vinegar	1 tablespoon chopped fresh parsley
1/2 teaspoon salt	olive oil
1 clove garlic, minced	optional: 1 tablespoon virgin olive oil
1 tablespoon freshly cut chives	

Wash eggplant well and cut into cubes. Heat olive oil in a skillet and cook eggplant cubes, stirring frequently, until wilted. Drain and set aside in a bowl to cool.

Add vinegar, salt, garlic, herbs and additional olive oil, if desired. Toss well and chill for at least 4 hours.

YIELD: 6 SERVINGS

WILD RED PEPPER SOUP

2 cups chopped sweet red peppers	1 teaspoon freshly grated lemon peel
1 cup chopped onion	3 tablespoons flour
3 tablespoons olive oil	1 1/2 cups water
1 1/2 pounds tomatoes, peeled and chopped	3 tablespoons butter or margarine
1 teaspoon salt	sour cream
freshly ground pepper to taste	parsley

Sauté onions and peppers in olive oil until tender. Add tomatoes and simmer for 10 minutes. Place in blender with water and spin quickly until blended but not completely smooth.

Melt butter in saucepan and stir in the flour to make a roux. Add soup gradually and whisk to blend; simmer gently for another 10 minutes. Add lemon peel, salt and pepper.

Serve steaming hot, topped with a spoonful of sour cream and some chopped parsley in the center of each bowl.

YIELD: 6 SERVINGS

JAPANESE EGGPLANTS
WITH MISO AND CHICKEN SAUCE

Japanese eggplants are a miniature form of the vegetable that the English blamed for causing madness when it reached their country in the sixteenth century. They shunned it, though we think they must have been mad to pass up its culinary potential. These little eggplants make good appetizers, and their skin is more tender than that of the larger varieties.

You can make the chicken sauce ahead of time and do the eggplant just before serving. This makes an unusual first course. You may have to go to an Oriental specialty store to get the bean paste and the sake.

1/4 pound boneless skinless chicken breast (about half a small breast)
2 tablespoons sendai miso (dark bean paste)
1 tablespoon sugar
3 tablespoons sake (Japanese rice wine)
2 tablespoons Chicken Broth (page 145)
1 pound Japanese eggplants vegetable oil
freshly ground pepper to taste
freshly snipped parsley

Freeze chicken breast for a few hours and then thaw for about 1/2 hour. Trim off any fat and cut into tiny cubes. Reserve.

Preheat oven to 400°F.

Mix bean paste, sugar, sake and chicken broth in a small saucepan. Bring to a boil, them simmer, stirring, for several minutes.

Add chicken to bean sauce and simmer until chicken turns white. Continue cooking gently for a few minutes to blend the flavors.

Cut unpeeled eggplants in half lengthwise without removing stems. Brush cut surface with oil and place, cut side down, in a shallow baking dish. Bake for 10 minutes; turn and bake cut side up for 5 minutes more, or until flesh is tender. Run briefly under the broiler to brown. Spread sauce lightly over eggplant halves and serve with a sprinkle of pepper and parsley.

YIELD: 4 SERVINGS

CAROLE EITINGON'S
CALIFORNIA SALSA

California salsa is more like a finely-chopped salad than a sauce, though if you wish a smoother consistency you can add a small amount of tomato sauce. Fresh cilantro is not to everyone's taste, so modify the amount or even delete it if you like. This is a good recipe for low-salt diets: It's so highly flavored that it needs no salt or pepper. If you can't find fresh jalapeño peppers, buy the bottled kind and use six to twelve slices, chopped.

6 to 8 plum tomatoes, chopped
1/2 green pepper, diced
1/2 red pepper, diced
1/2 cucumber, peeled and diced
6 scallions, chopped, including green part
1 clove garlic, minced
1/4 cup chopped fresh cilantro
1 small jalapeño pepper (or to taste), seeded and chopped
2 tablespoons olive oil
2 tablespoons red wine vinegar
1/4 fresh lime, squeezed

Combine all ingredients and serve over fish or omelets, or with tortilla chips and guacamole.

LINGUINI WITH
RED PEPPERS AND SCALLOPS

4 tablespoons olive oil
2 large red peppers, chopped
1½ pounds bay scallops
¼ cup flour
2 large cloves garlic, minced
1 cup Chicken Broth (page 145)

juice of ½ lemon
½ teaspoon salt
freshly ground pepper to taste
⅓ cup freshly snipped parsley
1 pound linguini

Boil water for pasta.

In a large frying pan, heat 2 tablespoons of the oil and sauté peppers for 2 to 3 minutes over medium-high heat, until barely tender. Remove with a slotted spoon and set aside.

Toss scallops with flour. In the same frying pan, heat remaining olive oil and sauté scallops, stirring constantly, for 2 minutes. Add garlic and cook for 2 minutes more, or until scallops turn opaque. Remove with slotted spoon and set aside.

Pour broth into frying pan, bring to boiling point, and deglaze the pan. Remove from heat. Add lemon juice, salt, pepper and parsley. Return peppers and scallops to pan and set aside.

Cook linguini according to package directions. Reheat scallop and pepper mixture if necessary. Drain pasta well and pour into serving bowl. Add scallops and peppers to dish and toss well. Serve immediately.

YIELD: 6 SERVINGS

PIZZA WITH PESTO,
EGGPLANT AND RED PEPPERS

Dough for 1 12-inch pizza
   (page 147)
1 1-pound eggplant
salt
¼ cup olive oil
Approximately ⅓ cup Pesto
   (page 146)

1 small red pepper, chopped
½ pound mozzarella cheese,
   grated
2 ounces Parmesan cheese,
   grated

Peel eggplant and cut into 1-inch cubes. You will have about 4 cups of cubes. Place in a strainer over a bowl, sprinkle with salt, toss and let stand for an hour to drain.

In the meantime, prepare dough according to recipe on page 147 and let rise.

Discard eggplant juices and pat cubes dry with a paper towel. Heat olive oil in a large skillet and sauté cubes over medium-high heat for 6 to 8 minutes, stirring constantly, until they are lightly browned and tender. Set aside.

When dough has risen, preheat oven to 450°F., roll out dough and place in pan according to recipe. Spread surface of crust with *pesto* and top with eggplant cubes and pepper. Sprinkle with cheeses. Bake for 20 to 25 minutes, or until crust and cheeses are golden brown.

YIELD: 4 SERVINGS (2 SLICES APIECE)

STIR-FRIED CHICKEN WITH PEPPERS AND SNOW PEAS

3 whole boned chicken breasts, cubed	about 2 pounds
4 tablespoons peanut oil	1/4 pound snow peas, trimmed
2 large cloves garlic, minced	1/4 cup bottled Chinese oyster sauce
1 large yellow pepper, cored and cubed	1 tablespoon soy sauce
1 large red pepper, cored and cubed	1 tablespoon sesame oil
1/2 cup raw split cashew nuts	

You can substitute any number of green vegetables for the snow peas: small broccoli florets; inch-long pieces of asparagus, cut on the diagonal; even quartered Brussels sprouts.

Cut chicken into cubes; set aside.

Heat 2 tablespoons of the oil in a wok or large frying pan and sauté cashew nuts over fairly high heat until golden brown. Remove with slotted spoon and set aside.

Add chicken to wok and stir-fry just until cubes turn white. Remove and set aside.

Add remaining oil to wok, heat and add vegetables. Stir-fry over fairly high heat for 2 minutes. Return chicken and cashews to wok and add remaining ingredients. Toss together for 1 minute and serve immediately with rice.

GRILLED MAKO SHARK WITH ROASTED YELLOW PEPPER PURÉE

Other varieties of shark (black-tip, et cetera) and swordfish make perfectly good substitutes if you can't get mako shark. For that matter, you can use other colored peppers, particularly red or orange.

2 large yellow peppers, about 1 pound	salt and freshly ground pepper to taste
1 large clove garlic	2 pounds mako shark steaks
1 tablespoon balsamic vinegar	fresh parsley for garnish

Place one pepper on a long metal fork and roast directly over a medium gas flame or under a broiler, turning as it chars so that it is blackened on all sides, including top and bottom. Place in a paper bag, close loosely, and repeat with second pepper. Let peppers steam in bag for at least five minutes.

When peppers are cool enough to handle, peel and scrape off the charred skin under running water. Cut peppers in half lengthwise and remove the cores, seeds and veins. Cut flesh into cubes.

Place cubes in a blender with garlic, vinegar, salt and pepper, and blend until completely smooth. (You can use a food processor but you will not get as fine a purée.) Pour the mixture into a small saucepan.

Season shark steaks to taste and grill or broil, turning once, until steaks are cooked but still moist (time will vary according to thickness of steaks). Just before serving, bring purée to a simmer. To serve, place a spoonful or 2 of pepper purée on each plate adjacent to a portion of fish and garnish with a sprig of parsley.

Eaten in moderation, red hot peppers are said to be beneficial to the digestion, but they can also be "rubefacient" (in plain English, causing the skin to blush a deep red). Varieties containing a small amount of capsaicin, an oily orange substance that lines the inner veins, are only mildly hot; with others better endowed it is recommended that you keep a fire extinguisher handy.

PASTA PRIMAVERA WITH YELLOW PEPPERS

4 tablespoons (¹/₂ stick) butter or
   margarine
1 cup heavy cream
1¹/₂ cups freshly grated Parmesan
   cheese
salt and white pepper to taste
1 small bunch broccoli
2 cloves garlic, minced
1 small zucchini, sliced

1 cup peas
2 large yellow peppers, cut into
   2-inch strips
10 large mushrooms, sliced
1¹/₄ cups corn oil
1 pound rotelle or other spiral
   pasta
¹/₂ pint cherry tomatoes, halved

Heat water for pasta.

In a heavy saucepan, melt butter and add cream and 1 cup of the Parmesan cheese. Heat until cheese has melted, stirring constantly. Remove from heat, season to taste and set aside.

Cut broccoli into bite-sized florets and save stems for another use. Prepare other vegetables.

In a large skillet or wok, heat oil and stir-fry broccoli, garlic and zucchini for 2 minutes over moderately high heat. Add remaining vegetables and continue to stir-fry until they are barely tender, but still crisp. Remove from heat.

Boil pasta according to package directions to desired consistency. Drain. Add tomatoes to vegetables and heat until warmed through. Reheat sauce if necessary. Toss sauce and vegetables with pasta in a large serving bowl, adding remaining grated Parmesan.

YIELD: 8 SERVINGS

PEPERONATA WITH SAUSAGE

Serve peperonata as a main dish with spaghetti.

2 tablespoons butter or margarine
¹/₄ cup olive oil
¹/₂ cup chopped onion
1³/₄ pounds sweet peppers of
   various colors, seeded and
   chopped
1 pound plum tomatoes, coarsely
   chopped

2 cups Fresh Tomato Sauce
   (page 146)
1 tablespoon red wine vinegar
1 teaspoon salt
freshly ground pepper to taste
2 cups peas
1 pound Italian sweet sausage,
   broiled
1 pound spaghetti

Bring water for pasta to a boil.

Heat 1 tablespoon each of the butter and the olive oil in a skillet and sauté onion until soft and lightly browned. Add remaining butter, oil and peppers, reduce heat, cover and cook for 5 minutes, stirring occasionally. Add tomatoes, tomato sauce, vinegar, salt, pepper and peas, and cook 5 minutes more.

Slice cooked sausages, add to skillet, and simmer together for a final 5 minutes.

Cook spaghetti al dente, according to package directions. Drain. Place on large, rimmed serving dish and toss with peperonata

YIELD: 6 SERVINGS

Everyone agrees that pumpkins and squash, those uniquely American vegetables, are from the same botanical family, *Cucurbitaceae.* All further distinctions as to which varieties belong to which branch, however, get lost in a hopeless tangle of taxonomical confusion. The word "squash," from the Narragansett Indian *Askooot-asquash,* seems to be an umbrella term incorporating pumpkins and sometimes even the inedible gourds; as Tom Stobart writes in *The Cook's Encyclopedia,* "They all have a fruit which, however variable, is built on the same general plan."

The confusion began with the sixteenth-century Spanish and French explorers to the New World, who wrote back describing "melons" since they had nothing else to compare them with in

PUMPKINS & SQUASHES

Europe. These vegetables were among the very first to be cultivated by American Indians, who used them along with maize and beans as the keystone of their diet. Although we tend to think of pumpkins largely in terms of Halloween jack-o'-lanterns, the Indians were extremely resourceful, using them to make everything from soups and stews to bread and candy. They also deep fried the blossoms, roasted the seeds and sometimes used the shell as a casserole. The Pilgrims picked up these traditions, serving pumpkin pie, it is said, at the first Thanksgiving feast in 1621. They even figured out a way to

make beer from pumpkins when their early attempts at growing barley and hops proved disappointing.

The United Fresh Fruit and Vegetable Association, not generally known for its whimsy, advises that the selection of a pumpkin "depends on whether it's for eating or for scaring people." Pumpkins can get as heavy as two-hundred pounds, but the ideal size for cooking is the three-to-five-pound sugar pumpkin. It should have a good golden-orange color, a hard rind, be free of bruises and heavy in relation to its size.

Botanical squabbles aside, the easiest way to classify the remainder of the edible squash family is into summer and winter squashes. The former, harvested when unripe, when the skin is tender and the seeds immature, include the crookneck and straightneck yellow squash; the scalloped white pattypan; some of the softer-skinned varieties of the turban squashes, shaped exactly as they sound; and, of course, zucchini. Winter squashes grow more slowly and are harvested late in the season when their shells are hard enough to protect the pulp inside through several months of storage. They provide us with some of the more wonderful shapes among vegetables: the curvaceous butternuts; the bumpy Hubbards; the corrugated round acorns; and the flamboyant Turk's turbans.

Summer squash should be firm, shiny and relatively unblemished. *The Cook's Encyclopedia* advises that they are too old to eat when a fingernail can't penetrate their skin without pressure. The best zucchini are no more than six inches long and 1½ inches in diameter. But those few that escape picking in the zucchini patch, hidden by leaves, and grow to gargantuan proportions, you can always grate and freeze in batches, using them later in casseroles and breads. Winter squash should have no softness of rind and should be heavy for their size. They are generally sweeter, tastier and more nutritious than the summer varieties.

When pumpkin is out of season, any winter squash may be substituted in this unexpected and delicious ravioli. One three-pound pumpkin yields about one and a half pounds peeled flesh, or two cups of purée. This makes a spectacular luncheon—or a lovely first course when your main dish is a light one. In the latter case, serve only three or four ravioli per person.

1 3-pound pumpkin	*1 1-pound package egg roll*
1 tablespoon heavy cream	*wrappers*
1 tablespoon butter or margarine	*1 egg, lightly beaten*
2 tablespoons minced fresh sage	*2 large shallots, minced*
2 teaspoons minced fresh thyme	*1 tablespoon butter or margarine*
1/2 teaspoon salt	*1 tablespoon flour*
white pepper to taste	*2 cups Chicken Broth (page 145)*
	salt and white pepper to taste

Cut a "lid" in the top of the pumpkin, open and scoop out all the loose pulp and seeds. Divide pumpkin into 6 or 8 pieces and pare off the outer skin. Cut into smaller chunks and steam for 10 to 15 minutes, or until tender.

Purée pumpkin in a blender or food processor. Add cream, butter, corn-meal, half the sage, half the thyme, salt and white pepper. Mix well.

Place 1 egg roll wrapper on a flat surface and brush it with beaten egg. Place 1 heaping teaspoonful of purée in the middle of each quarter of the sheet—4 mounds per sheet. Place another sheet of pasta exactly on top of the first, pressing down lightly all around each mound from the center out to the edges.

With a crimping wheel, trim a small border off each outer edge. Use the crimper to cut the 4 squares apart, so that all four sides of each square have the crimped pattern. Place formed ravioli on a tray or baking sheet. Continue in the same way until all pasta sheets are used.

Bring a large pot of water to boil so it will be ready for the pasta. Make the sauce: In a large frying pan, melt butter and sauté shallots until wilted. Add flour and cook over low flame for a minute or 2, stirring constantly.

In a separate pot bring broth to a boil. Gradually add broth to butter mixture and stir vigorously until sauce thickens a little. Add remaining sage and thyme, and salt and pepper to taste. Set aside. When water is boiling, add half the ravioli, bring back to a boil, and cook over high flame for 4 to 5 minutes or until pasta is tender. Remove with slotted spoon to a strainer, drain carefully, then slide into sauce in frying pan. Bring water back to a boil and cook the other half the same way. When ready to serve, bring sauce just to a boil and serve ravioli napped with sauce in big shallow soup dishes.

YIELD: 30 TO 40 LARGE RAVIOLI

A miracle of packaging is the pumpkin. "How many foods, after all," asks Betty Fussell, "come in their own pots? All of it—from blossoms and shell to seeds and meat—is useful, thanks to Yankee (or Indian) thrift.

Acorn squash are members of the winter squash family, dating back to several centuries B.C. in Central America. Grown in summer and harvested in fall, the family earns its name by lasting all through the winter, since the squash are picked when fully mature and therefore hard shelled.

SPAGHETTI SQUASH WITH CHARLOTTE'S SAUCE

This is truly one of nature's miracles: The apparently solid flesh of this squash shreds into crunchy, spaghettilike threads when it is cooked. If you want to bake the squash, you can cut it in half lengthwise, scoop out the seeds and bake it, cut side down, in a pan containing two inches of water for about twenty minutes in a 350°F. oven. Boiling the squash, however, is easier (see directions below). If you want to cook the squash ahead of time, you can reheat the strands in aluminum foil in a 350°F. oven for about ten minutes while you are making the sauce.

1 large spaghetti squash	½ cup grated Parmesan cheese
½ cup (1 stick) butter or margarine	salt and freshly ground pepper to taste
1 cup sour cream	3 small scallions, diced, including green part

Boil water in a pot large enough to hold the squash. Prick squash in several places with a long fork and place in boiling water. When water returns to a boil, cover, lower heat and simmer for 20 to 30 minutes, until a fork can easily pierce the flesh. Remove from water and cool.

Split squash in half lengthwise and scoop out the seeds and stringy pulp. With the tines of a fork, "rake" the flesh away from the shell to form spaghettilike strands. You should have 6 to 8 cups. Place in a bowl and set in a warm place.

In a small saucepan, melt butter, whisk in sour cream and add Parmesan cheese. Heat to melt cheese but do not let mixture boil. Add salt and pepper.

In a serving dish, toss spaghetti squash with sauce and garnish with scallions.

YIELD: 6 SERVINGS

ACORN SQUASH STUFFED WITH WILD RICE, PECANS, AND RAISINS

3 large or 4 small acorn squash	salt to taste
butter or margarine	1 cup wild rice
brown sugar	½ cup raisins
salt	1 tablespoon dried basil
freshly ground pepper	⅓ cup chopped pecans, lightly toasted
3 cups Chicken Broth (page 145)	

Preheat oven to 350°F.

Cut acorn squash in half crosswise and scoop out seeds. Shave a little off pointed ends so each half can sit flat in the pan.

Place cut side down in a shallow baking dish. Gently pour about an inch of boiling water into dish. Bake for 45 minutes.

Turn cut side up. Into each cavity put 1 tablespoon butter and 1 tablespoon brown sugar. Sprinkle with salt and pepper. Bake 15 minutes longer.

While squash is cooking, prepare wild rice: Bring broth to a boil. Add salt and wild rice, cover and simmer for 30 minutes. Add raisins and basil and simmer 15 to 20 minutes more, or until rice is just tender. Toss with pecans.

Divide rice mixture among cavities of cooked squash and serve.

YIELD: 6 TO 8 SERVINGS

MARION SCHACHER'S
ZUCCHINI CASSEROLE

1 onion, minced	2 large zucchini, grated (about
1 shallot, minced	5 cups)
3 tablespoons butter or margarine	1/2 cup grated Gruyère cheese
1/2 pound mushrooms, sliced	1/2 cup heavy cream
salt, freshly ground pepper and	bread crumbs
ground nutmeg to taste	additional grated cheese

Preheat oven to 350°F.

Sauté onion and shallot in butter until translucent. Add mushrooms and sauté until wilted. Sprinkle lightly with salt, pepper and a pinch of nutmeg. Grate zucchini and squeeze as dry as possible through cheesecloth. Add to mushroom mixture and heat through. Sprinkle with grated cheese and stir until cheese melts. Add cream and continue cooking until warmed. Transfer to a buttered casserole and sprinkle with bread crumbs and additional cheese. Bake uncovered for 1/2 hour.

YIELD: 4 TO 6 SERVINGS

PENNY FLEMING'S
SPAGHETTI SQUASH PRIMAVERA

This is a great way to use vegetable leftovers and create the illusion of a completely new dish. Almost any combination of vegetables will do as long as they are not overcooked. If you're in a hurry and have a microwave, you can cut the squash in half lengthwise, scoop out the seeds, place the squash cut side up in a pan with a quarter cup water, cover with plastic wrap, and cook on "high" for eight minutes.

1 large spaghetti squash	1 cup broccoli florets
2 tablespoons butter or margarine	1/4 cup pine nuts, lightly toasted
1/2 cup chopped red pepper	1 cup Fresh Tomato Sauce (page
1/2 cup chopped yellow pepper	146)
1 cup sliced mushrooms	optional: grated Parmesan cheese
1 cup peas	

Boil water in a pot large enough to hold the whole squash. Prick squash in several places with a long fork and place in boiling water. When water returns to a boil, cover, lower heat and simmer for 20 to 30 minutes, until a fork can easily pierce the flesh. Remove from water and cool.

Split squash in half lengthwise and scoop out the seeds and stringy pulp. With the tines of a fork, "rake" the flesh away from the shell to form spaghettilike strands. You should have 6 to 8 cups. Set aside.

Melt butter in a small frying pan and sauté the peppers, mushrooms and peas for a few minutes until crisp-tender. Steam broccoli in a separate pan. In a saucepan, toss squash with all other vegetables, pine nuts and tomato sauce. Heat just until warmed through. Serve with grated Parmesan cheese, if desired.

YIELD: 6 TO 8 SERVINGS

VEGETABLE LASAGNA
WITH TWO SQUASHES

If you don't have green beans, you can substitute other cooked and leftover vegetables such as broccoli or cauliflower. Keep the pieces small.

1 large red pepper
1 small zucchini
1 small yellow squash
2 tablespoons olive oil
2 cups sliced fresh mushrooms
2 carrots, peeled and coarsely grated
1½ cups peas
1 cup cooked green beans, chopped

3 cups Fresh Tomato Sauce (page 146)
9 lasagna strips
2 pounds ricotta cheese
1 pound mozzarella cheese, half frozen and then coarsely grated
2 eggs, lightly beaten
½ cup grated Parmesan cheese

Core and seed red pepper, then chop. Scrub squashes, cut in half lengthwise, then slice thinly.

In a large frying pan, heat oil and sauté pepper, squashes and mushrooms only until mushrooms yield their juice. Add other vegetables and toss quickly to heat through. Add 2½ cups of the tomato sauce, reserving ½ cup.

Cook lasagna according to package directions and drain. Run pasta under cold water, drain again, and lay flat in a single layer on paper towels until needed.

Preheat oven to 350°F.

Combine ricotta, mozzarella and eggs and set aside.

In a 9- x 13-inch baking dish, spread a few tablespoons of the remaining tomato sauce on bottom of pan. Cover with a layer of lasagna. Spread half the ricotta mixture on top, followed by half the vegetable mixture. Repeat the layers, ending with lasagna. Spread the few remaining tablespoons of plain sauce on top and sprinkle with Parmesan cheese.

Cover with aluminum foil and bake for 20 minutes. Uncover and bake for 5 minutes more.

YIELD: 6 TO 8 SERVINGS

SWEET SQUASH SOUFFLÉ

If you want to gild the lily, you can serve this Light Almond Custard (page 99) or a strawberry purée (page 135).

2 pounds winter squash, peeled,
   seeded, and cut in chunks
2 teaspoons plus 3 tablespoons
   butter or margarine
3 tablespoons flour
1 cup milk, brought to a boil
1/2 teaspoon salt

3 tablespoons sugar
1/2 teaspoon nutmeg
1/2 teaspoon cinnamon
4 egg yolks
5 egg whites, at room temperature
1/4 teaspoon cream of tartar

Steam squash until tender, about 20 minutes. Remove from pan and purée in a food processor or blender. Spoon purée into a large piece of cheese-cloth; wrap cloth around squash and squeeze to remove as much moisture as possible. Measure out 3/4 cup and set aside.

Preheat oven to 400°F. Grease a 6-cup soufflé dish with 2 teaspoons butter. Roll sugar around in it to coat bottom and sides and shake out excess. Melt remaining butter in a heavy 2 1/2-quart saucepan, stir in flour, cook over moderate heat for 2 minutes. Remove from heat, pour in boiling milk, and stir with a wire whisk until thick and smooth. Beat in sugar, nutmeg and cinnamon. Return to heat and simmer for a minute or 2, then remove from heat and beat in egg yolks, 1 at a time. Stir in the puréed squash.

Beat egg whites until foamy. Add cream of tartar and resume beating till whites stand in stiff peaks. Stir several big spoonfuls of egg whites into the squash mixture, then gently fold in remaining whites.

Pour soufflé mixture into buttered dish and smooth the top with a spatula. Set on middle rack of oven and immediately turn heat down to 375°F. Bake for 25 to 30 minutes (do not open oven door), until soufflé puffs up above rim of dish and top is nicely browned.

YIELD: 4 SERVINGS

B.J.'s PURÉED MAPLE SQUASH

1 medium-sized butternut squash
1 tablespoon butter or margarine

1 tablespoon maple syrup
pinch of ground cloves

Peel the rind from a butternut squash, cut in half and remove the seeds. Cut into chunks. Steam until tender but not mushy.

Place in a food processor or blender with butter or margarine, maple syrup and cloves. Process until smooth. Serve immediately, or place in an oven-proof pot in a warm oven until serving time.

YIELD: 4 SERVINGS

MAUDE ARCHIBALD'S ZUCCHINI BREAD

3 eggs	1 teaspoon salt
1 cup vegetable oil	1 teaspoon baking soda
1½ cups sugar	1 teaspoon baking powder
2 cups grated, unpeeled zucchini	1 tablespoon cinnamon
1 tablespoon vanilla	optional: raisins, nuts, dates
3 cups flour	

Preheat oven to 350°F.

Thoroughly beat together the eggs, oil and sugar. Add the grated zucchini and the vanilla.

In another bowl, mix the flour with salt, baking soda, baking powder and cinnamon. Make a well in the center and add the zucchini mixture and raisins or nuts if desired. Stir thoroughly, but not to the point where the mixture becomes heavy.

Pour into 2 well-buttered loaf pans and bake for 1 hour.

YIELD: 2 LOAVES

PUMPKIN DATE-NUT MUFFINS

It's fun to start from scratch, using a whole pumpkin, especially if you have some help or at least some company in the kitchen. But if you're not up to it, this is one recipe where it won't make a big difference if you substitute two cups of canned, unspiced pumpkin purée.

1 3-pound pumpkin	1 teaspoon baking powder
10 tablespoons (1¼ sticks) butter	1 teaspoon baking soda
or margarine	½ teaspoon ground cloves
1½ cups sugar	1 teaspoon cinnamon
4 eggs	½ teaspoon salt
⅔ cup water	¾ cup chopped dates
2½ cups sifted flour	¾ cup chopped pecans

Cut a "lid" in the top of the pumpkin, open and scoop out the loose, soft pulp and the seeds. Divide pumpkin into 6 or 8 pieces and pare off the outer skin. Cut into smaller chunks and cook in a steamer for 10 to 15 minutes, or until tender. Purée in a blender or food processor.

Preheat oven to 400°F.

Cream butter and sugar until light and fluffy. Add eggs and beat thoroughly. Stir in 2 cups pumpkin purée and water and beat well.

Sift flour with baking powder, baking soda, cloves, cinnamon and salt. Carefully fold into liquid ingredients, mixing just until dry ingredients are moistened. Stir in dates and nuts. Fill well-greased muffin tins almost completely full.

Bake for 20 minutes, or until toothpick inserted in center comes out clean.

YIELD: 24 MUFFINS

"What brings back the past, like the rich pumpkin pie?" asks John Greenleaf Whittier. A late nineteenth-century housewife recalls a pretty vignette from the pumpkin fields high up in the Sierra Nevada: "It is a fine sight to watch the harvesting of such a field. The big fruits roll down the slopes just like golden balls. Men stand below, with sacks ready, to receive them..."

This delicious and unusual recipe comes from the *Foothills Trader*, a Northwestern Connecticut weekly of which Mrs. Ludlam is the publisher. As with the pumpkin muffins, you can use canned pumpkin purée in this recipe if the fresh is not available—or if you're not.

2/3 cup white sugar	1/4 teaspoon salt
1/4 cup water	5 eggs
3/4 cup brown sugar	1 1/2 cups whole milk or half-and-
1 cup pumpkin purée	half
1/2 teaspoon cinnamon	2 teaspoons vanilla
1 teaspoon ginger	optional: 2 tablespoons chopped
1/2 teaspoon nutmeg	crystallized ginger or 4 to 5
	knobs preserved ginger, sliced

Combine white sugar and water in a heavy large-bottomed frying pan. Cook over medium heat until the sugar melts. Then increase the temperature and continue cooking. Watch carefully and remove as soon as the mixture turns a medium brown. Pour it into a 9-inch pie dish, tipping the dish to coat the bottom.

Preheat oven to 350°F.

In a large bowl, combine brown sugar, pumpkin, cinnamon, ginger, nutmeg and salt. In a smaller bowl, beat eggs, milk and vanilla together until thoroughly blended. Combine the 2 and mix well. Pour this custard on top of the caramel.

Set the pie dish inside a larger pan. Pour water in the larger pan until it comes 3/4 way up the sides of the pie dish. Bake for 50 to 60 minutes, or until a knife blade inserted in the middle comes out clean.

Cool, then chill.

To serve, run a knife around the edge of the custard, then invert onto a large, shallow serving dish. The caramel will pour down the sides. If desired, decorate with chopped or sliced ginger.

YIELD: 8 SERVINGS

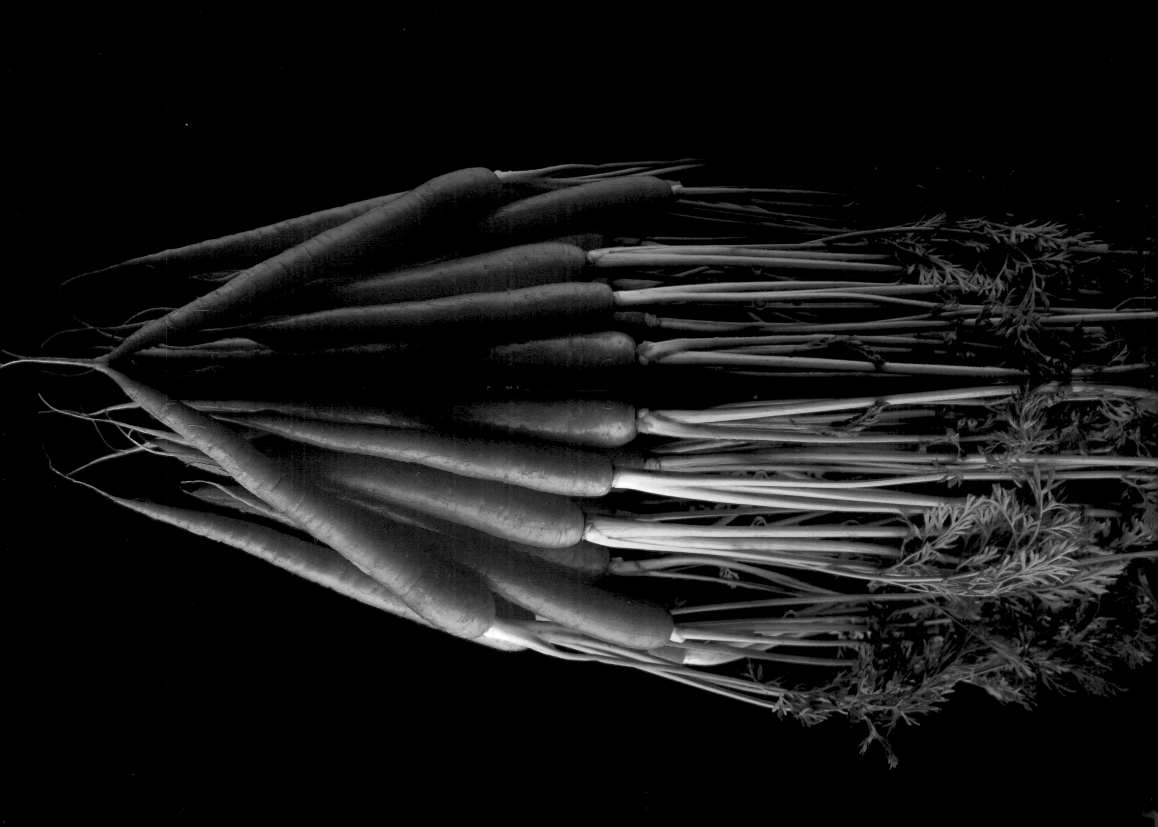

The root vegetables aren't much to look at, but their unlovely skins hide a multitude of subtle and pleasing flavors. Although most of them are available year round, they are especially welcome in the winter when, in many parts of the country, we have few choices of fresh produce. When cooked in creamy purées and satisfyingly thick soups and stews, root vegetables are the comfort food of the season.

The most popular in this group is probably the carrot, perhaps because it has more sugar than any other vegetable except beets. Its leaves are the clue to its affiliation—the parsley family—and you may be surprised to learn that when carrots grow wild, by the roadside, they're called Queen Anne's lace. The Greeks used carrots as

CARROTS, PARSNIPS, POTATOES, TURNIPS & BEETS

a "love medicine," a category in which they also included the snout and foot of the hippopotamus.

Closely related is the parsnip, whose taste offers a hint of its tie to the parsley family. Oddly enough, though this wonderful and aromatic vegetable is rarely served today, it was eaten more widely than carrots in the Middle Ages. It's a winter vegetable that gets sweeter the later it is harvested although the biggest ones may develop a woody core. Both carrots and parsnips should be firm, smooth and

uncracked, and parsnips should not have any discolored patches.

Potatoes had a terrible time gaining acceptance. Originating in South America, they were initially rejected in North America and Europe and used only for animal fodder or ornamental plants. Skeptics warned that they were powerful sex stimulants, and caused leprosy, and in any case should be avoided because they were not mentioned in the Bible. By the eighteenth century, most countries had recognized the potato's potential for feeding the poor and preventing famine, even if Brillat-Savarin in 1825 still dismissed it as "eminently tasteless." Potatoes became the staple food of Ireland, but when the crop failed in 1845, it created the Great Potato Famine, a disaster of epic proportions.

Today, of course, world potato production is almost up there with wheat. There are three basic categories: new potatoes, good for boiling; general purpose potatoes; and baking potatoes, also good for frying. (Sweet potatoes, by the way, are tubers of a completely different family and of tropical American origin.) All potatoes should be firm and smooth with as few irregularities as possible.

In the curious and shifting balance of vegetable popularity, turnips have been cultivated and used as food in Europe since Greek and Roman times—even if they were not particularly admired—but they are probably the most maligned and ignored of vegetables today. (Their yellow cousin, rutabagas, not mentioned anywhere before the seventeenth century, are probably a mutant.) The Greeks and Romans also ate the leaves of the beet, and it was not until sometime around the beginning of the Christian era that someone discovered that the roots tasted pretty good, too.

If you're lucky enough to find turnips or beets in the market with their tops still intact, the freshness of the leaves is a good indicator of quality. You can sauté the greens as a separate dish with a little oil and garlic. Otherwise, select the roots as you would their relatives: firm and smooth.

SPECKLED CREAM OF PARSNIP SOUP

YIELD: 4 TO 6 SERVINGS

2 tablespoons butter or margarine
1 onion, chopped
1 pound parsnips
1 large clove garlic
4 cups Chicken Broth (page 145)
1/2 teaspoon dried tarragon leaves
1 carrot, grated
salt and freshly ground pepper to taste
1/2 cup heavy cream
1/2 teaspoon dried basil leaves

Melt butter in a stockpot and sauté onion until translucent.

Peel and chop parsnips and garlic and toss with onion. Cover, lower flame and cook for 10 minutes.

Add broth and herbs and simmer, covered, for 10 minutes more or until parsnips are completely tender. Purée in a food processor and return to pot, adding grated carrot. Cook gently for several minutes until carrot loses its bite. Stir in seasonings and cream and serve immediately.

BABY NEW POTATOES STUFFED WITH SOUR CREAM AND CAPERS

YIELD: ABOUT 35 POTATOES

2 pounds baby new potatoes, about 1 1/2 inches in diameter
1 3 1/2-ounce bottle of capers
1/2-cup sour cream
1 tablespoon freshly snipped parsley
sprinkle of salt

Preheat oven to 400°F.

Select potatoes, as far as possible, of uniform size. Scrub them, cut a small "X" in the top of each potato, and bake for 30 minutes or until cooked through.

In the meantime, drain capers well and mix gently with sour cream, parsley and salt. When potatoes are done, remove from oven and let cool for 15 minutes. With a melon baller, scoop out a little hollow in the top of each potato. Spoon in caper mixture and serve.

This makes a nice, hearty hors d'oeuvre, or it can serve 6 to 8 people as a side dish with fish, steak or roast beef.

"The parsnip, children, I repeat/Is simply an anemic beet," wrote the late poet Ogden Nash, but we can't let that slander rest. For one thing, parsnips are from the carrot family; for another, they have a lovely, distinctive flavor, sweet and nutty. Nash, however, was apparently unmoved. Grumbled he: "Some people call the parsnip edible/Myself, I find this claim incredible."

SCOTCH BROTH

The lamb stock for this recipe should be made the day before you plan to serve it so it can be degreased. The stock takes about three hours to cook. This is a main-course soup.

Stock

4 pounds lamb meat and bones	1 bay leaf
10 cups water	1/2 teaspoon dried thyme
2 tablespoons salt	freshly ground pepper to taste

To prepare stock: place lamb, water and seasonings in a stock pot. Simmer slowly for 3 hours.

Strain through a cheesecloth; remove the meat from the bones, shred it and set it aside. Cool stock and refrigerate overnight. You should have about 2 quarts.

Soup

4 tablespoons (1/2 stick) butter or margarine	3 tablespoons flour
1 onion, chopped	3 large carrots, sliced
1 large clove garlic, chopped	2 parsnips, sliced
1 cup chopped celery	2 turnips, diced
1/2 cup barley	2 cups shredded cabbage

The next day, melt butter and sauté onion, garlic and celery for 5 minutes without browning. Add barley and flour and cook 2 minutes more, stirring well. Skim fat from lamb stock and pour stock over vegetables, mixing well. Add carrots, parsnips and turnips and simmer slowly for an hour.

Add cabbage and shredded lamb meat and simmer 30 minutes more.

YIELD: 8 SERVINGS AS A MAIN COURSE

BASIL VICHYSSOISE

3 cups peeled, sliced potatoes	salt and white pepper to taste
3 cups sliced leeks, white and light green parts only	2 cups loosely packed fresh basil leaves
6 cups Chicken Broth (page 145)	1 cup heavy cream

Simmer potatoes and leeks in broth for about 30 minutes, or until tender. Add salt, pepper and basil and cook just until leaves are wilted.

Purée the soup (in batches, if necessary) in a food processor or blender. Add cream, stir and correct seasoning. Cool, then chill.

YIELD: 8 SERVINGS

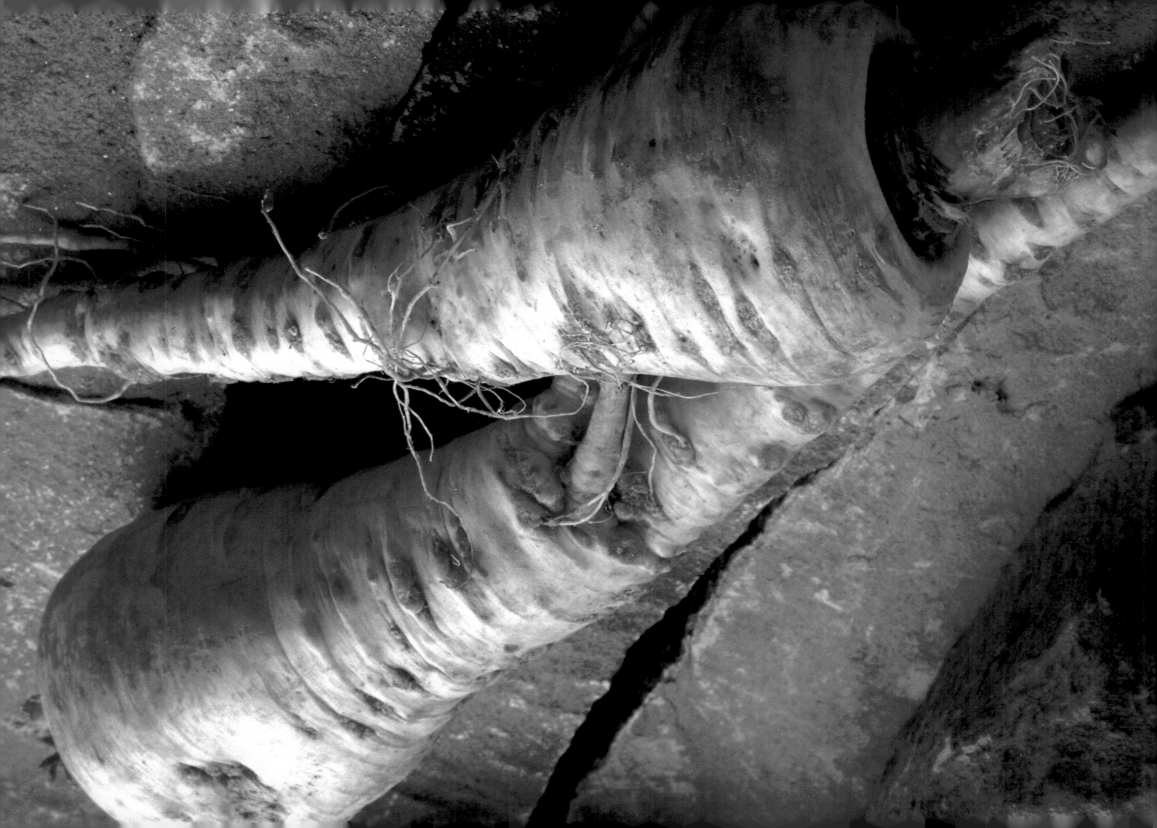

''RED SPINACH''

This was my father's favorite vegetable dish; he coined the name because the texture reminded him of creamed spinach. Steaming is the most convenient cooking method for beets. They lose too much color and flavor in boiling, and baking takes too long. If fresh beets are not in season or you're pressed for time, you can use a one-pound can of cooked beets, drained. And slightly less milk.

2 bunches beets (about 1¼
   pounds when stemmed)
1 tablespoon butter or margarine
1 teaspoon flour
1 cup hot milk

½ teaspoon salt
2 tablespoons fresh lemon juice
1 teaspoon sugar
freshly ground pepper to taste

Trim beet stems to 1 inch and leave the tips intact, so the beets will "bleed" as little as possible during cooking. Washing gently, being careful not to tear the skin. Steam for 45 minutes over boiling water; beets are done when a fork easily pierces them or when skins loosen easily to the touch

Cool beets slightly, then run under cold water and slip off the skins. Trim if necessary at stem or tip end. Put beets through the grating disk of a food processor, or chop finely by hand in a wooden bowl. Set aside.

In a saucepan large enough to hold the beets, make a white sauce: Melt butter, and add flour, whisking constantly over a low flame for a minute or 2 so flour gets cooked. Gradually add hot milk and whisk until sauce begins to bubble and thicken. Add salt, lemon juice, sugar and pepper and blend well.

Fold beets into sauce and mix well. Taste to correct seasoning.

YIELD: 4 SERVINGS

WINTER VEGETABLE MEDLEY

This robust vegetable dish goes well with simple roast beef or lamb.

4 medium white turnips, cubed
2 medium carrots, sliced thickly
1 large parsnip, sliced lengthwise
   and then crosswise
florets from 1 head broccoli
1 cup peas
3 tablespoons butter or margarine
½ onion, minced
3 tablespoons flour

2½ cups hot milk
¾ teaspoon salt
freshly ground pepper
½ teaspoon thyme
1 small bay leaf
pinch of nutmeg
2 scallions, chopped, including
   green part

Cook turnips and carrots in boiling salted water for about 4 minutes; add parsnip, broccoli and peas, and cook for 7 minutes more. Drain quickly and keep vegetables warm while preparing sauce.

In a saucepan, melt butter. Add onion and sauté until transparent. Stir in flour and cook for a few minutes more. Gradually add hot milk and whisk until sauce begins to bubble and thicken. Add seasonings and simmer, stirring, for about 5 minutes.

Place vegetables in a serving dish and pour over them just enough sauce to cover. Shake until evenly coated and sprinkle with scallions. Serve immediately.

YIELD: 6 TO 8 SERVINGS

WARM POTATO SALAD WITH BACON AND RADISHES

3 pounds medium potatoes	2/3 cup chopped scallions, including green part
6 bacon slices, chilled	1 cup sliced radishes
1 tablespoon flour	2 tablespoons chopped parsley
1/2 cup white vinegar	1 1/2 teaspoons salt or to taste
1/2 cup water	freshly ground pepper to taste
4 tablespoons sugar	

Cook potatoes in boiling water until tender, about 30 minutes. Drain, cool, peel and cut into cubes.

While potatoes are cooking, cut chilled bacon slices into small pieces. Sauté over low heat until crisp. With slotted spoon, remove bacon and set aside on paper towels.

Drain from skillet all but 1 tablespoon of bacon fat and stir in flour until smooth. Gradually add vinegar and water and stir in sugar; bring to boiling point, stirring.

In a serving bowl toss potatoes lightly with bacon, scallions, radishes and parsley. Season with salt and pepper. Add warm dressing and blend gently; serve immediately.

YIELD: 6 TO 8 SERVINGS

SCANDINAVIAN BEET AND HERRING SALAD

Matjes is young herring—the word, in fact, means "little girl" or "virgin" in Dutch. These first herring of the season are lightly cured in brine and have a slightly sweet taste. This is a fairly substantial salad that works well as a luncheon dish served with soup and black bread.

1 cup diced cooked beets	1/4 cup minced scallions, including green part
1 cup pared, cored and diced apples	3 tablespoons red wine vinegar
2 medium potatoes, cooked and diced	salt and freshly ground pepper to taste
1 cup diced matjes herring	1/2 cup heavy cream, lightly whipped
1/2 cup finely diced dill pickles	

To cook beets: leave on root ends and about 1 inch of stems. Wash gently but well and steam for 45 minutes over boiling water, until fork-tender. Run under cold water and slip off skins. Dice.

Gently mix beets with all remaining ingredients except cream. Then fold in the lightly whipped cream. The beets will turn everything pink. Cover bowl and chill for several hours. Just before serving, correct seasoning if necessary.

YIELD: 6 SERVINGS

Three or four centuries ago, the beet was considered something of a cure-all for yellow jaundice and many other illnesses. Anglo-Saxons used the root to make a bone salve, and an emetic; they recommended its juice as a remedy for festering wounds and infections bites.

SWEET POTATO-TANGERINE PUDDING

This pudding is a perfect companion for roast poultry—and the tangerine is a welcome relief from marshmallows.

3 pounds (about 8 to 9) sweet
    potatoes
5 tablespoons butter or
    margarine, melted
8 tablespoons brown sugar, firmly
    packed

¹/₄ cup dark rum
¹/₄ teaspoon nutmeg
¹/₂ teaspoon salt
5 tangerines
3 tablespoons chopped pecans

Wash sweet potatoes and boil, unpeeled, in water to cover until soft, about 20 minutes. Drain well, cool, peel and mash.

Add 3 tablespoons of the butter, 6 tablespoons of the sugar, the rum, nutmeg and salt, and blend until mixture is smooth.

Preheat oven to 350°F.

Peel tangerines and remove the white membranes. Cut the sections from three of the tangerines in halves, removing the seeds. Fold into the sweet potato mixture. Turn into a buttered 2-quart casserole.

Puncture the centers of the remaining tangerine sections to remove the seeds. Arrange in an attractive design on top of the pudding.

Combine the remaining sugar and butter with the pecans. Sprinkle over the top and bake at 350°F. for 30 minutes.

YIELD: 6 TO 8 SERVINGS

CARROT PIE

This tastes a little like a pumpkin pie, but the color is brighter and the texture is lighter.

pastry for a 9-inch deep-dish pie,
    partially baked (page 148)
2 pounds carrots
2 tablespoons butter or margarine
¹/₃ cup pure maple syrup

grated rind of one small lemon
2 eggs
¹/₂ teaspoon cinnamon
¹/₂ teaspoon nutmeg
¹/₂ teaspoon ground ginger
1 cup heavy cream

Preheat oven to 450°F.

Pare carrots, slice thinly, and steam for 15-20 minutes or until tender. Purée in a blender or food processor. Stir in butter, maple syrup, and lemon rind.

When cool, beat in eggs, then add spices and cream. Pour into pie shell and bake for 10 minutes. Lower heat to 300°F. and bake for about 45 minutes more, or until firm.

YIELD: 6 TO 8 SERVINGS

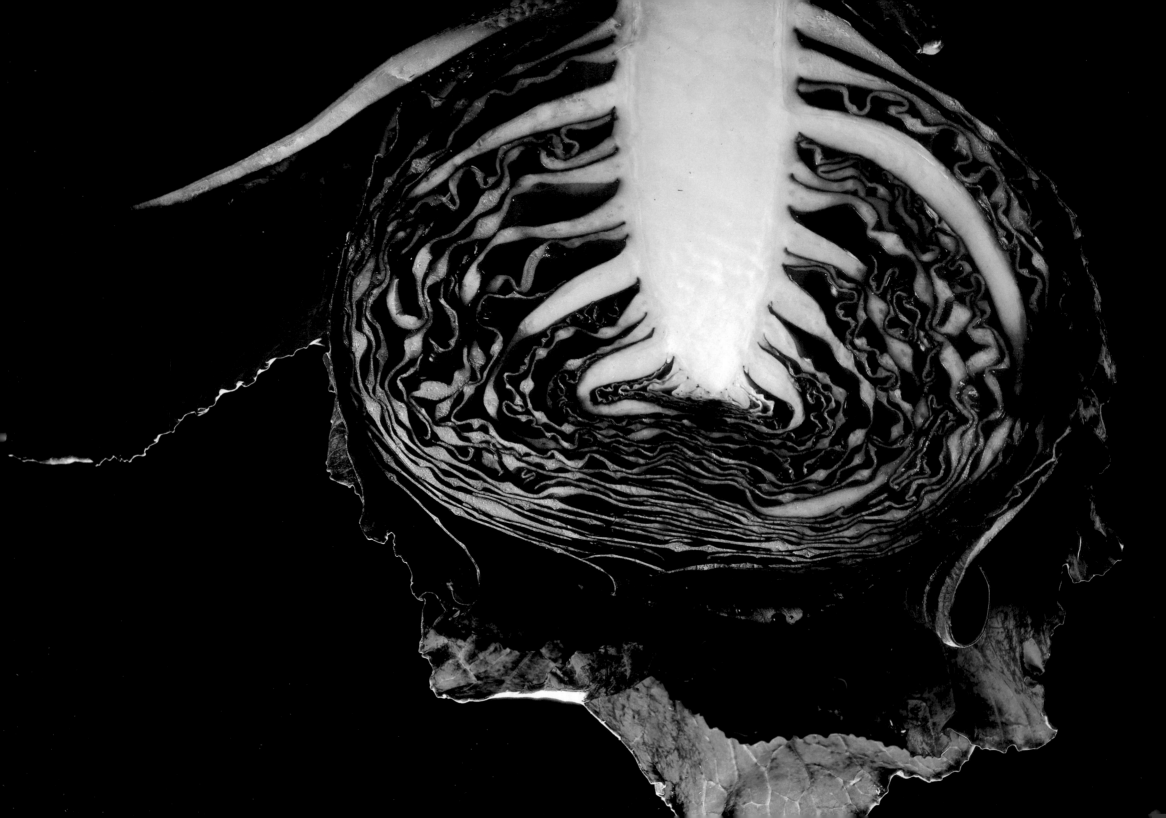

An ancient Greek myth described a Thracian king, Lycurgus, caught in the act of pulling up grapevines by the god of wine, Dionysos. The king, fearing the punishment of the raging god," wept profusely. When those tears fell to the ground, they were said to produce the first cabbage. This most ancient of vegetables has, in turn, produced some pretty bizarre offspring, including Brussels sprouts and kohlrabi as well as broccoli and cauliflower.

Called "man's best friend in the vegetable world," cabbage is from the mustard family and is exceptionally high in vitamin and mineral content. The Greeks held it in great favor as a hangover remedy; Roman demand initially made cabbage too expensive for

CABBAGE, BROCCOLI & CAULIFLOWER

the poor; and Rabelais exulted, "Oh thrice and four times happy those who plant cabbages!"

Not everyone, of course, was so enamored. Jane Grigson mutters about cabbages having "a nasty history of being good for you," and says, "as a vegetable it has original sin, and needs improvement." And a lovely collection of food quotations called *Consuming Passions,* edited by Jonathon Green, catches turn-of-the-century journalist Walter Page in a double slur (vegetable and ethnic) when he says, "The English have only three vegetables—and two of them are cabbage."

Red cabbage was not known until the Middle Ages. The Chinese varieties, on the other hand, are ancient, but are botanically confusing since they were greatly improved by American growers after World War I and returned to China in altered states. When buying any form of cabbage except the loosely-formed bok choy, look for solid, compact, heavy heads with a minimum of outer "wrapper" leaves. All varieties should be crisp and well colored.

By developing the flower element of cabbage, horticulturists produced both broccoli and cauliflower. Popular in Greece and Italy for some two thousand years, broccoli turns up in the first-century writings of Pliny. Tiberius reportedly had to restrain his son from losing his head over the cooked broccoli of the gourmet Apicius. The United States came late to this enthusiasm and although broccoli was grown at Williamsburg and Monticello, it wasn't common on American tables until the 1920s.

Cauliflower, which Mark Twain has memorialized by calling it "a cabbage with a college education," is just that: another advanced form of cabbage. Many reference books attribute its "education" to the Orient, whence it migrated to the Romans. It was so enjoyed in eighteenth-century France that Louis XV named a cauliflower dish after his mistress, Madame du Barry. Once again, Americans turned up their noses, but given the overcooked, watery or poorly seasoned state to which so many of them subjected it, it's no wonder that generations of children have grown up to despise the vegetable.

It has taken this last decade, with its emphasis on healthy vegetables and quick-cooking methods, to restore the popularity of both broccoli and cauliflower. When you buy them, look for firm heads of good color. Avoid broccoli that has turned yellow or begun to flower, and speckled or spotted cauliflower that can indicate insect damage, mold or decay. There is a purple variety of both broccoli and cauliflower that makes a gorgeous table decoration but that loses virtually all of its color in cooking.

RHODA SCHNEIDER'S
CAULIFLOWER SOUP

Garnish this soup with finely chopped chives or parsley, slivered carrot, or a dab of sour cream.

2 tablespoons butter or margarine	1 cup light cream
1 large onion, chopped	1/4 teaspoon nutmeg
4 cups Chicken Broth (page 145)	salt and freshly ground pepper to taste
2 medium-sized carrots, sliced	optional: fresh chives for garnish
1 head cauliflower, cut into small pieces	

In a large pot melt butter and sauté onion for about 5 minutes, or until tender but not brown. Pour in chicken broth and bring to a boil. Add vegetables, reduce heat, cover and simmer until tender, about 8 minutes.

Purée in small batches in a blender or food processor until smooth. Return purée to pot and stir in cream and seasonings.

Heat to simmering and serve hot; or let cool and refrigerate to serve cold. Garnish with chives.

MARY EITINGON'S
CABBAGE PIROSHKIS

These can be served as hors d'oeuvres, or as an accompaniment to a hearty main-dish soup.

1/2 cup (1 stick) butter or margarine	2 tablespoons butter or margarine
1 3-ounce package cream cheese	2 hard-boiled eggs
1 1/4 cups flour	salt and freshly ground pepper to taste
2 1/2 cups shredded cabbage (tender leaves only)	1/4 cup freshly snipped dill
1 large onion, chopped	1 egg yolk

Preheat oven to 400°F.

Mix butter, cream cheese and flour together with fingers or pastry blender until mixture resembles coarse meal. Knead until dough will form a ball, but do it rapidly to avoid losing flakiness. Chill for at least 1 hour.

In the meantime, cook cabbage in boiling water for 10 minutes; drain. Sauté onion in butter until transparent, add cabbage, and cook for 10 minutes more or until moisture has evaporated. Chop or put briefly in food processor with hard-boiled eggs and seasonings. Cool thoroughly.

When dough has chilled, divide it into 3 or 4 balls. Roll each out on a floured board to 1/8-inch thickness. Using a glass with a 3 1/2-inch diameter, cut out rounds of dough.

Place a rounded teaspoon of cabbage filling in the center of each round. Wet rim of dough slightly with water, fold in half and pinch to seal, forming "half-moon" pouches.

Place sealed side down on greased baking sheets. Beat egg yolk with a few drops of water and brush top of each pouch. Bake for 20 minutes or until golden brown.

Among the ancients, cabbage was valued as a remedy against drunkenness. The Egyptians ate it before drinking wine at banquets; the Greek commentator Eubulus wrote of its virtues with respects to hangovers: "Wife, quick! some cabbage boil, of virtues healing/That I may rid me of this seedy feeling."

Chinese cabbage is a confusing term that covers both the tightly packed, yellow-white celery cabbage and the more loosely-growing bok choy with its larger, dark green leaves. Mentioned in Chinese works as early as the fifth century, this long cabbage is as refreshing an accompaniment to Western-style meals as it is an integral part of Chinese menus.

CHINESE CABBAGE AND PORK DUMPLINGS

This recipe is a lot of work—but you can make a satisfying meal of it if you serve it with a Chinese soup or the Celery-Flavored Winter Tonic on page 70.

1½ cups very finely chopped Chinese cabbage	1 tablespoon sesame oil
1 pound lean, boneless pork, finely ground	¾ cup cold water
	2 cups sifted flour
1 tablespoon finely chopped, peeled fresh ginger root	3 tablespoons peanut oil
	1 cup Chicken Broth (page 145)
1 large clove garlic, minced	¼ cup soy sauce
1 tablespoon soy sauce	2 tablespoons white vinegar

Squeeze cabbage in a kitchen towel to extract as much moisture as possible. Mix well with pork, ginger, garlic, soy sauce and sesame oil and store in refrigerator.

Add water to flour gradually, mix well, and knead until smooth. Cover with damp towel and let rest for 20 minutes.

Knead again briefly. Divide dough into 2 parts, and roll each into a cylinder about an inch wide and 12 inches long. Cut cylinder into ½-inch slices, sprinkle each slice lightly with flour, and flatten with the heel of your hand.

With a lightly floured rolling pin, roll each slice into a 3-inch circle. Place a tablespoon of pork and cabbage filling in the center of each round, fold in half, and pinch or pleat edges to seal. Keep finished dumplings on a lightly floured cookie sheet covered with a dry towel while you proceed with the rest.

Heat 2 tablespoons of peanut oil in a 12-inch skillet to 375°F. Place dumplings in pan with pleated side up and sides touching, and cook over low heat for 2 minutes or until bottoms are lightly browned. Add chicken broth, cover pan and cook over moderate heat for 10 minutes, until liquid has entirely evaporated.

Add remaining tablespoon of oil to pan and fry dumplings uncovered on the unbrowned side for another 2 minutes. Mix soy sauce and vinegar to make a dipping sauce. Serve immediately.

YIELD: 48 DUMPLINGS

BROCCOLI AND CHICKEN SALAD

1 3-pound chicken	1 bunch broccoli
1 onion, peeled and split	1¼ cup Garlic Mayonnaise (pages 145-46)
2 carrots, trimmed and peeled	
2 ribs celery, trimmed	1 pint yellow or red cherry tomatoes
6 sprigs parsley	
salt and freshly ground pepper to taste	Finely chopped parsley for garnish

Combine the chicken, onion, carrots, celery and parsley in a large pot. Add salt and pepper and water to cover. Bring to a boil. Partly cover and simmer 45 minutes or until chicken is completely tender. Let chicken cool in broth.

Remove chicken from pot, discard skin and bones and cut the chicken meat into bite-sized pieces.

Cut the broccoli into small florets; trim the stalks and cut into small lengths. Steam over boiling water until barely tender—do not overcook. Cool

Cut cherry tomatoes in half.

Combine chicken, broccoli, cherry tomatoes and mayonnaise in a serving bowl and toss gently to blend. Before serving, sprinkle with chopped parsley.

YIELD: 6 SERVINGS

BROCCOLI-CHEESE SOUFFLÉ

1 bunch broccoli
2 teaspoons plus 4 tablespoons butter or margarine
3 tablespoons plus 1/2 cup extra-sharp Cheddar cheese, grated
2 to 3 shallots, minced
4 1/2 tablespoons flour
1 1/2 cups milk, brought to a boil
3/4 teaspoon salt
1/8 teaspoon pepper
optional: dash of mace
6 egg yolks
7 egg whites, at room temperature

Cut broccoli into florets. Trim stalks and cut into short pieces, splitting any that are thicker than 1 inch. Steam for about 10 minutes, or until just tender. Drain well and dice to make 1 1/4 cups. Reserve any remaining broccoli for another use.

Preheat oven to 400°F.

Butter the inside of an 8-cup soufflé mold with 2 teaspoons of the butter. Sprinkle with 3 tablespoons of the cheese.

Melt the remaining butter in a heavy large saucepan and sauté shallots until transparent. Stir in flour and cook over moderate heat for 2 minutes without browning. Remove from heat, pour in boiling milk and stir with a wire whisk until thick and smooth. Beat in seasonings. Return to heat and simmer a minute or 2, then remove and beat in egg yolks, 1 at a time. Stir in the diced broccoli and taste to check seasonings.

Beat egg whites with a pinch of salt until stiff. Stir 1/4 into the sauce base, then stir in the remaining grated cheese. Gently fold in remaining egg whites and pour into prepared soufflé dish. Set on middle rack of oven. Immediately turn heat down to 375°F. and bake for 40 minutes or until a knife inserted in the center comes out clean.

YIELD: 6 SERVINGS

FETTUCCINE WITH CAULIFLOWER, MULTICOLORED PEPPERS AND PESTO

If you can't find every color pepper for this recipe, improvise!

3 tablespoons vegetable oil
1 tablespoon salt
1 head cauliflower
1 each; red orange, yellow, green and purple peppers, seeded and chopped
2 cups peas
1 pound fettuccine
1 cup Pesto (page 146), at room temperature
Freshly grated Parmesan cheese

Boil water for pasta, adding 1 tablespoon each of oil and salt.

Cut cauliflower into bite-sized florets. Steam over boiling water for about 5 minutes, or until crisp-tender. Set aside.

Heat 2 remaining tablespoons of oil in large skillet and add chopped peppers and peas. Sauté for about 5 minutes, stirring, until vegetables are crisp-tender. Add cauliflower and toss to blend; remove from heat.

Cook fettuccine according to package directions until al dente. Drain and place in a large pasta bowl. Add pesto and blend well. Add vegetables and toss briefly. Serve immediately with Parmesan cheese.

YIELD: 6 SERVINGS

Cauliflower: not loved by everyone, but oh, so good for you. Its nutritive riches include a heavy dose of folic acid, a B vitamin used to treat ane-mia. This has led health-food enthusiasts to call it "vegetable liver," which has probably hastened its decline in popularity. Cauli-flower also has rich stores of calcium and iron, valuable to those who can't drink milk.

BROCCOLI STIR-FRY WITH RED PEPPERS AND WATER CHESTNUTS

1 bunch broccoli	salt and freshly ground pepper to taste
1 large red pepper	½ cup Herb Vinaigrette (page 145)
3 tablespoons corn oil	1 8-ounce can of water chestnuts, drained
1 large garlic clove, minced	

Cut broccoli into uniform bite-sized florets with about 2 to 3 inches of stalk.

Core pepper and cut into rings, then shorter strips.

Heat the oil in a wok or large frying pan until very hot. Add broccoli (it should sizzle) and stir-fry for 5 minutes.

Add vinaigrette, garlic, red pepper and water chestnuts and stir-fry for another 3 minutes. Season to taste and serve immediately.

YIELD: 4 SERVINGS

CABBAGE WITH SOUR CREAM AND DILL

1 small onion	1 tablespoon sugar
2 tablespoons butter or margarine	3 tablespoons vinegar
1 small head cabbage, shredded	1 egg, beaten
salt and freshly ground pepper to taste	1 cup sour cream
	2 tablespoons freshly snipped dill

Sauté onion in butter until translucent. Add the cabbage and cook, covered, until tender but not browned.

Mix together egg, sour cream, sugar, vinegar, salt, pepper and dill. Pour over cabbage and heat but do not allow mixture to reach the boiling point. Serve immediately.

YIELD: 6 SERVINGS

Since red cabbage is tougher than the green varieties, it must have a longer cooking time over a slow, gentle flame. But beware of overcooking, which makes the cabbage mushy and too strong. All its color will wash out unless you cook it with an acid such as vinegar or lemon juice, which preserves its glorious purple hue.

INSALATA BIANCA

The chef at a fancy French restaurant once sent the waiter back to my table, complaining that my order was "too white." With that in mind, serve this salad as part of a salad buffet at a summer (or winter) luncheon, along with other more colorful offerings such as Scandinavian Beet and Herring Salad (page 50), Tabbouleh (page 25), Marinated Eggplant Cubes with Fresh Herbs (page 28) and Cucumber Salad Mizeria (page 74).

1 small cauliflower, cut into florets
1 small fennel bulb, diced
1 6-ounce jar artichoke hearts, marinated in olive oil, drained
4 large mushrooms, sliced
2 small boiled potatoes, peeled and diced
3 tablespoons wine vinegar

1¹/₂ tablespoons Dijon mustard
9 tablespoons imported olive oil
¹/₂ teaspoon salt
freshly ground pepper to taste
¹/₂ cup Mayonnaise (pages 145–46)
3 anchovy fillets, diced
1 tablespoon chopped capers

Steam florets over boiling water for about 5 minutes, or until crisp-tender. Drain and cool. Combine with other vegetables.

Blend vinegar with mustard; add olive oil gradually while stirring with wire whisk. Add salt and pepper. Stir in mayonnaise, anchovies and capers. Blend gently with vegetables and chill.

YIELD: 8 to 12 SERVINGS

B.J.'S RED CABBAGE COLE SLAW

You can make this simple and delicious cole slaw using more or less mayonnaise and sour cream, depending upon size of cabbage, as long as they are mixed in equal proportions.

1 medium-sized red cabbage
1 cup Mayonnaise (pages 145-46)

1 cup sour cream
2 teaspoons caraway seeds

Remove the hard core from the cabbage and shred finely. Mix together other ingredients, toss with cabbage and chill.

YIELD: 8 SERVINGS

Ah, the onion family—joy of our tastebuds and bane of our neighbors and loved ones. It may have been their lusty smell and taste that attracted the ancients to gather these bulbs in the first place. In the first century A.D., a Martial epigram noted, "He who bears chives on his breath/Is safe from being kissed to death," and a sixteenth-century writer, Thomas Nashe, proclaimed, "Garlick hath properties that make a man winke, drinke, and stinke."

According to Waverley Root, a Turkish legend has it that when Satan was cast out of heaven, "garlic sprouted where he first placed his left foot and onions where he placed the right." The onion family has been cultivated for so long that its wild ancestors are simply

ONIONS, GARLIC, SHALLOTS, SCALLIONS & LEEKS

unknown. We do know that it belongs to the lily family and has played a starring role in almost every cuisine on earth.

Reactions to these bulbs have always been as strong as their flavor. Pliny tells us that the onion was an object of worship in ancient Egypt—one has even been found in the hand of a mummy. Robert Louis Stevenson called it "rose among roots" (perhaps he was thinking of the sweet and mild red onion?). On the other hand, the Brahmins in India forbade the onion's consumption among their members, and the Pompeian guild of fruit and vegetable vendors conspicuously excluded the onionmongers, who had no choice but to form a separate, lowlier association.

Perhaps no vegetable has been assigned as many miraculous properties as garlic. It is said to ward off hay fever and witches, give stamina to athletes and livestock, cure frostbite and backaches, soothe dog bites and ulcers. In fact, recent scientific studies have demonstrated that a chemical in garlic reduces the risk of heart attack and stroke; and that garlic consumption both diminishes cholesterol and has protective value against cancer and diabetes. News stories in 1977 hailed the development of an odorless strain of garlic by a Japanese horticulturist, but since it hasn't yet appeared on the market one would have to assume that it turned out to be a flop.

Shallots and scallions have been mixed up and used interchangeably by botanists, food historians and consumers alike. When you ask for shallots, you generally get the delicately flavored lavender or brown-skinned little bulbs that come singly or in clusters, and taste like a cross between onion and garlic. Scallions, on the other hand, come in bunches and are a form of young, green onions with long, green tubular leaves.

Leeks, the national vegetable of Wales and sometimes called "poor man's asparagus," are so hardy they can survive winter underground. An Assyrian herbal says they will keep your hair from turning gray, something even garlic can't claim.

Onions, shallots and garlic should be hard and well shaped, with skins that are papery, and with no sign of seedstems and sprouts. Green onions should have green, fresh tops and white portions that extend for two or three inches above the root.

SKORDALIA (GREEK GARLIC SAUCE)

This sauce is traditionally served with fried or broiled fish, boiled beets, fried eggplant, or zucchini. But it also works well as a dip for crudités. It is extremely pungent and can be modified by using less garlic.

5 cloves garlic
2 cups sliced, cooked potatoes (about 3 medium-sized potatoes)
1 1/2 tablespoons wine vinegar
juice of 1 lemon
1 egg yolk
1 teaspoon salt
3/4 cup olive oil

Peel and crush garlic. Combine all ingredients in a blender and blend until completely smooth.

LEEK AND POTATO PIE

At last! *This* is what to do with leftover mashed potatoes.

1 10-inch deep-dish unbaked pie shell made with Basic Pie Pastry (page 148)
3 large leeks
2 tablespoons butter or margarine
1 pound cottage cheese
2 eggs
2 cups mashed potatoes
1/2 cup sour cream
1 1/2 teaspoons salt
generous pinch of cayenne pepper
3 tablespoons freshly grated Parmesan cheese

Preheat oven to 425°F.

Cut roots and tops off the leeks, leaving 2 inches of leaves. Wash thoroughly, cut into rings, and rinse again. Sauté leeks in butter for about 5 minutes, or until wilted.

In electric blender or food processor, place cottage cheese and eggs and blend until smooth. Place in large bowl and add mashed potatoes. Stir well, and then beat in sour cream, salt and cayenne. Stir in leeks.

Spoon into pastry shell and sprinkle with grated cheese. Bake for 50 minutes, or until golden brown. Cut into slices and serve.

YIELD: 8 SERVINGS

For centuries, garlic has been prescribed for everything from backaches and epilepsy to frostbite and scorpion stings. A head of garlic hung on the bedroom door is supposed to guarantee the birth of a baby boy. But did you know that it could stave off vampires? Wear a cluster of this miracle herb around your neck and fear no more.

GARLIC CHICKEN ON SKEWERS

It's much easier to cube chicken when it is very, very cold. Put chicken into the freezer for about an hour before you prepare this dish. After the marinade has been used, you can remove the onion slices with a slotted spoon. Sauté them until lightly browned and serve as an accompaniment to the chicken.

¹/₄ cup freshly squeezed lemon juice	*1 large onion, sliced*
¹/₂ cup olive oil	*3 large cloves garlic, crushed*
1 teaspoon salt	*2 tablespoons finely chopped parsley*
freshly ground pepper to taste	*4 whole boneless chicken*
¹/₂ teaspoon oregano	*breasts, partially frozen*

In a glass or stainless steel bowl, whisk together the lemon juice, oil, salt, pepper and oregano. Add the onion, garlic and parsley, mixing well.

Cut chicken into large cubes. Toss in dressing. Let stand for 8 to 10 hours in the refrigerator.

Preheat broiler. Thread chicken on skewers and place on a rack in a broiler pan with shallow sides. Broil 3 inches from the heat for about 3 minutes on each side, or until chicken is just cooked through and is getting nicely browned on the outside.

YIELD: 4 TO 6 SERVINGS

SHALLOT BUTTER

Here's one recipe where margarine is really not an acceptable substitute for butter. This makes a wonderful topping for steaks, hamburgers, potatoes and many vegetables.

¹/₂ cup (1 stick) cold butter	*salt and freshly ground pepper to taste*
1 tablespoon minced shallots	
2 tablespoons freshly snipped parsley	*1¹/₂ tablespoons lemon juice*

In electric mixer, cream butter until light and fluffy. Add shallots, parsley, salt and pepper. Beat in lemon juice slowly until absorbed. Chill.

POOR MAN'S CIOPPINO

Traditional cioppino, a San Francisco fisherman's specialty with Italian overtones, contains the best of the day's catch and usually includes more elaborate seafood such as crab and shrimp. This is a scaled-down version with pasta. Scallops are a good substitute if bass or weakfish are not available, and of course you can always use fresh basil and oregano.

¼ cup olive oil	1 teaspoon dried oregano
1 large onion, chopped	1 teaspoon salt
1 green pepper, chopped	freshly ground pepper to taste
4 cloves garlic, minced	1 pound boned striped bass,
1 28-ounce can Italian tomatoes	sea bass or weakfish, cut in
3 tablespoons tomato paste	2-inch slices
1 cup red wine	3 pounds mussels, cleaned
½ cup chopped parsley	6 ounces (about 2½ cups) large
1 teaspoon dried basil	(not jumbo) shell noodles

Heat olive oil in a large Dutch oven and sauté onion, green pepper and garlic for about 5 minutes. Add tomatoes, tomato paste, wine, ¼ cup of the parsley, and the remaining seasonings. Bring to a boil, lower heat and simmer, covered, for 20 minutes.

Bring water for pasta to a boil in a separate pot.

Add fish and mussels to tomato sauce and simmer, covered, for about 10 minutes or until mussels have opened.

Cook noodles according to package directions; drain and mix with cioppino during last few minutes of cooking. Serve in large bowls with a pinch of remaining parsley in each.

YIELD: 6 SERVINGS

FRENCH-FRIED RED ONION RINGS

Allow one onion per serving, at least, since like popcorn, these are irresistible. Note that you need to soak the raw onion in milk for an hour, so leave yourself time.

4 red onions	flour for dredging
milk to cover (about 3 cups)	salt and freshly ground pepper to
oil for deep frying	taste

Peel onions and cut into ¼-inch slices. Cover with milk and soak for an hour. Drain and separate into rings. You may want to discard the tiny rings as they retain oil after frying and will be greasy.

Heat oil in a deep fryer with a strainer or in a large frying pan. Place flour and seasonings in a plastic or paper bag. Drop onion rings in batches into the bag and shake to coat. Remove and shake off excess flour.

Fry on high heat until golden brown. Remove and drain on paper towels. Season to taste and serve immediately.

YIELD: 4 SERVINGS

MIXED VEGETABLES WITH GARLIC AND CHEESE

As long as you have an interesting variety of tastes and colors, you can make any substitutions for the vegetables in this recipe.

1/2 large Bermuda onion, sliced	4 cloves garlic, crushed
1 cup peas	1/3 cup olive oil
1 10-ounce can beef broth	salt to taste
1 cup sliced carrots	1 bay leaf
1 cup sliced parsnips	1/2 teaspoon basil
1 small head broccoli, broken into florets	1/2 teaspoon tarragon
1 small head cauliflower, broken into florets	3 cups grated mozzarella cheese
1 small zucchini, sliced	1 cup freshly grated Parmesan cheese
1 cup fresh-cut green beans	3 tablespoons sesame seeds
2 medium tomatoes, cored and cut into eighths	
1 cup green pepper strips	

Preheat oven to 350°F.

Wash and cut all vegetables as indicated. Mix together in an ungreased shallow baking dish.

In a small saucepan, heat broth, garlic, olive oil, salt if desired, bay leaf, basil and tarragon. Bring mixture to a boil. Pour over vegetables.

Cover dish tightly with lid or aluminum foil and bake for 30 minutes, or until vegetables are just tender but still crisp. Remove aluminum foil and discard bay leaf.

Sprinkle with cheeses and sesame seeds, and place under broiler until cheese is melted but not brown. Serve immediately.

HERBED BARLEY SALAD WITH SCALLIONS

3 cups water	1 cup diced plum tomatoes
1 cup pearl barley	1 cup freshly snipped parsley
1/2 cup fresh lemon juice	1/2 cup minced scallions, including green part
1/2 cup olive oil	
1 teaspoon salt	
freshly ground pepper to taste	

This dressing is quite pungent—partly because the barley is so bland. If you prefer something milder, use one cup of the Herb Vinaigrette made with balsamic vinegar (page 145).

Bring water to a boil. Add barley and simmer until tender, around 45 to 55 minutes. Drain, rinse with cold water, and shake vigorously in a strainer to dry.

In a salad bowl, combine barley, parsley, scallions and tomatoes. Add lemon juice, oil, salt and pepper, and mix thoroughly. Chill.

YIELD: 6 TO 8 SERVINGS

Enough about the medical and mystical powers of garlic! Here is some practical advice: To remove the odor of garlic from your hands, wet them, rub them with table salt, rinse, then wash with soap. To freshen your breath, eat parsley.

Apparently bugs aren't crazy about the smell, either, so you can spray your vegetable garden with a natural insect repellent: Grind 4 garlic cloves and 3 hot chilies in a blender with 1 cup water; let stand 10 minutes, strain, and mix the liquid in a spray bottle with 5 more cups of water.

WHOLE-WHEAT ONION BREAD

This is an unusual and extremely convenient method for baking bread: The yeast starts to work in a twenty-minute period at room temperature, which takes the place of the usual "first rising." Then the dough rises in the refrigerator, leaving you free to go out or do something else until you're ready to bake it, anywhere from two to twenty-four hours later. It makes sensational toast.

1 medium red onion, finely chopped	4 teaspoons salt
3/4 cup minced fresh parsley	2 packages dry yeast
5 1/2 to 6 cups white flour	2 cups milk
2 cups whole wheat flour	3/4 cup water
3 tablespoons sugar	4 tablespoons (1/2 stick) butter or margarine

Prepare onion and parsley and set aside.

Combine flours. In the large bowl of an electric mixer, thoroughly mix 2 1/2 cups of the blended flours, sugar, salt and undissolved yeast by hand.

Combine milk, water and butter in a saucepan and heat gently until liquids are very warm (120°F. to 130°F.). The butter does not need to melt.

Gradually add liquids to flour and yeast mixture and beat 2 minutes at medium speed, scraping bowl occasionally. Add 1 more cup of blended flours and beat at high speed 2 minutes. Stir in onions (leaving a teaspoonful to sprinkle on top of the loaves), parsley and enough additional blended flour to make a stiff dough.

Turn out onto a lightly floured board and knead until smooth and elastic, about 8 to 10 minutes. Cover with plastic wrap, then a towel, and let rest 20 minutes.

Divide dough in half. Roll each half to a 9- x 14-inch rectangle. Beginning with a short side, roll each rectangle like a jelly roll and press gently to seal. Pinch ends and fold them under. Place each roll, seam-side down, in a greased 9- x 5- x 3-inch loaf pan. Brush loaves with oil, sprinkle with remaining onion bits and cover loosely with plastic wrap. Refrigerate the pans for 2 to 24 hours.

When ready to bake, preheat oven to 400°F. Remove pans from refrigerator and uncover; let stand at room temperature for 10 minutes. Puncture any gas bubbles that may have formed. Bake 35 to 40 minutes, or until done. (Remove one loaf from pan and tap bottom or sides; bread is done if it sounds hollow.) Remove loaves from pans and cool on wire racks.

YIELD: 2 LOAVES

GRILLED SCALLIONS

When you're grilling meat or fish outdoors, this is an easy and unusual accompaniment.

2 bunches plump scallions	1/2 cup Herb Vinaigrette (page 145)

Trim both ends of scallions and leave whole. Brush liberally with vinaigrette. Place directly on charcoal grill and barbecue 5 minutes on each side or until slightly charred and crispy. Serve as a side dish with grilled meat or fish.

YIELD: 4 SERVINGS

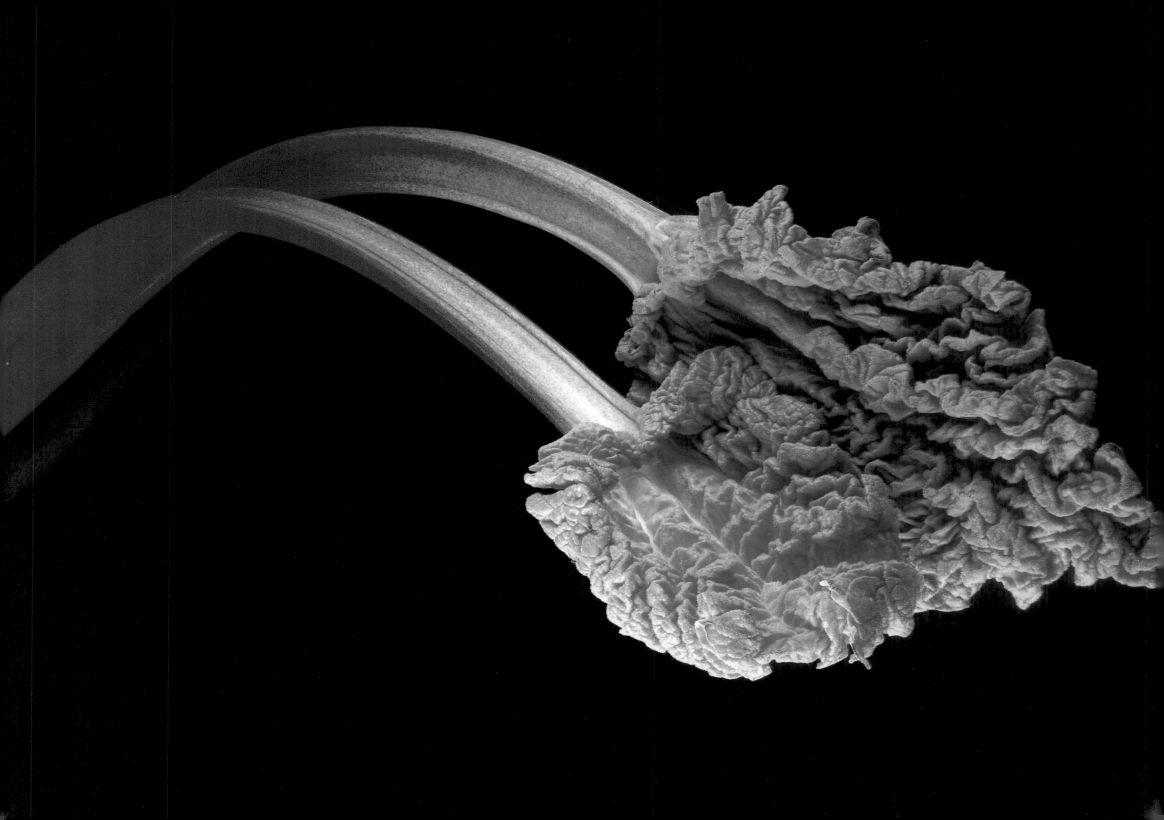

Rhubarb, Asparagus, Celery, Cucumbers and Corn. Any pretense of family connections or seasonal affinity comes to an end with this section. These items have only one thing in common: their length.

Actually, two: They are all vegetables, even rhubarb, though we persist in using it as a fruit. In fact, rhubarb's first recorded use was five thousand years ago in northern Asia, where the dried roots were used as a laxative and digestive. It took until the nineteenth century, for anyone to discover that the stalks were tasty. And there are still plenty of detractors. "Vegetable essence of stomach ache,' was Ambrose Bierce's definition, and Jane Grigson includes it only grudgingly in her *Fruit Book* because of nasty memories of it as

TALL THINGS

"Nanny-food" ("Good for you, dear") from her English childhood.

Good quality rhubarb stalks should be young and pink, firm but not woody. Thicker stalks tend to be tough and stringy. And caution! Never, never eat rhubarb leaves, which contain enough oxalic acid to be poisonous.

The devotees of the asparagus, a member of the lily family, go back at least to Greece and Rome. A fourth-century B.C. author warned that the vegetable caused blindness but others had more lascivious views. An Elizabethan writer, not unaware of its shape, thought it "manifestly provoketh Venus," and Madame de Pompadour mixed it with egg yolks to maintain her sexual vigor.

When you shop for asparagus, look for close and compact tips, and spears that are mostly green and still moist at the cut end. Find a market that sells asparagus loose, rather than in bundles, so you can pick out stems of the same size that will cook uniformly.

Yet another stalk is celery, from the parsley family, known in classical times. Wreaths of celery leaves were used to decorate tombs, to crown athletes, and, in Rome, to protect the heads they graced from hangovers. Waverley Root informs us that medieval magicians put celery seeds in their shoes in order to fly, but doesn't reveal their rate of success. Back to the stalks: When buying celery, think "crisp."

Cucumbers are from the same family as squash and melons. Recent carbon dating of seeds from the Burma-Thailand border has pushed their origins back to 7750 B.C. The Emperor Tiberius prized his cukes so highly that his gardeners raised them in beds mounted on wheels so they could be rolled out into the sunshine and back to shelter when the temperature dropped. A nineteenth-century folklorist proclaimed that dreaming of cucumbers meant you would speedily fall in love.

If not for corn, the Pilgrims might have starved to death. From friendly Indians, the colonists learned to plant corn and eat it, although they must have been amazed, as food historian Evan Jones puts it, at "the moving of cobs across hungry mouths like harmonicas." Those who put propriety above good eating still shuddered at the indelicacy. "Ladies should be particularly careful about how they manage so ticklish a dainty," wrote Charles Day in 1844, "lest the exhibition rub off a little desirable romance."

Sweet corn loses about 90 percent of its sugar to starch within the first hour of picking; hence the importance of cooking it right away. Don't even think about buying corn anywhere but a farmers' market. Look for fresh, green husks without any sign of worm injury or drying.

How cruel can April be if aspara-
gus is one of its gifts? These tender
green shoots were cultivated seri-
ously in ancient Rome, so much so
that reports have survived of aspar-
agus grown at Ravenna whose
stems weighed three pounds each.
One wonders at the time it must
have taken to cook them, surely it
would have contradicted a favorite
phrase of the Emperor Augustus,
"quicker than cooking asparagus."

ASPARAGUS-CHEESE TOAST

The best way to eat fresh asparagus, without question, is just plain or with a simple sauce. But once you've gotten that craving out of your system, here's a very tasty lunch or supper dish that is also an imaginative way to use leftover asparagus, if you ever have any. You can use this recipe for hors d'oeuvres if you spread the asparagus-cheese mixture on toast rounds or triangles rather than on whole slices of toast.

1/4 pound asparagus	2 teaspoons Worcestershire sauce
4 slices bacon	1 tablespoon tomato sauce
1 small onion, diced	freshly ground pepper to taste
1/2 pound sharp Cheddar cheese, grated	6 slices bread, toasted
	1 egg, beaten

Trim asparagus and cut diagonally into 1/2-inch pieces. You should have about 1 cup.

Cook bacon and drain well on paper towels. To bacon fat in frying pan, add onion and sauté until wilted, then add asparagus and stir-fry for 2 minutes, until crisp-tender. (If using leftover asparagus, slice it as directed above and do not cook any further.)

With a slotted spoon, transfer asparagus and onion to a mixing bowl, discarding as much bacon fat as possible. Cut cooked bacon into bits and add to bowl along with grated cheese.

In a separate smaller bowl, mix together beaten egg, Worcestershire sauce and tomato sauce. Pour into cheese mixture and blend well. Add pepper.

Preheat oven to 350°F.

Divide asparagus-cheese mixture evenly and spread on toast slices. Place on aluminum foil in a jelly-roll pan. Bake for 10 minutes, then place under the broiler briefly to brown the top.

YIELD: 3 SERVINGS

CELERY-FLAVORED WINTER TONIC

This is a nice way to use fresh tomato juice in the winter if your were clever enough to freeze some when cooking with garden tomatoes in the summer (see recipe for Fresh Tomato Sauce, page 146). If not, a good-quality canned juice will do. Orzo, small bits of pasta, can be found in many supermarkets. Serve this soup in glass bowls, if you have them, for a particularly attractive presentation.

2 cups consommé	1/4 cup sliced peeled shallots
2 cups tomato juice	1/2 cup cooked orzo or rice
3 cups sliced celery stalks and leaves	freshly snipped parsley to taste

Combine consommé, tomato juice, celery and shallots in a saucepan and bring to a boil. Simmer, covered, for 45 minutes or until celery pieces are very tender. You will have about 3 cups of broth.

Strain broth, pressing out as much of the vegetable essence as possible.

When ready to serve, reheat broth. Put a spoonful of orzo and a sprinkling of parsley in each dish and pour in the broth.

YIELD: 4 SERVINGS

RHUBARB KHORESH

This beef stew is an adaption of a Persian dish, actually a stewlike sauce served over rice. I've added more meat to suit American tastes.

1/4 cup flour
2 pounds lean stewing beef, cut in small cubes
4 tablespoons (1/2 stick) butter or margarine
1 large onion, finely chopped
1 teaspoon cinnamon
freshly ground pepper to taste
1 1/4 cups beef broth
1 pound rhubarb
1 tablespoon honey
salt to taste

Place flour in a plastic bag and lightly toss several pieces of meat at a time to dredge. Shake off excess.

In a large, heavy casserole or frying pan, heat 1 tablespoon of the butter until it sizzles and sauté half of the beef cubes until brown on all sides. Chunks of meat should not touch each other or they will steam instead of browning. Remove browned chunks with a slotted spoon, add another tablespoon of butter, and repeat procedure with the rest of the meat. Remove remaining meat.

Add another tablespoon of butter to pan, if necessary, and sauté onion until soft and golden. Sprinkle with cinnamon and pepper and cook for 1 minute more. Pour in broth and heat over low flame, stirring to loosen all browned bits on bottom of pan.

Return meat to pan and bring to a boil. Lower heat, cover and simmer gently for 1 1/2 to 2 hours, until meat is very tender.

Trim rhubarb stalks, wash and pat dry. Cut into 1 1/2-inch pieces. Sauté in remaining tablespoon of butter for a few minutes, then add to stew with honey. Simmer together for 10 minutes (do not overcook or rhubarb will disintegrate). Taste for seasoning and add salt if necessary.

YIELD: 6 SERVINGS

COLD CUCUMBER-HERB SAUCE

This sauce is very good with poached fish, any kind of shellfish, fresh tomatoes and avocados. It can also make a new meal out of leftover chicken: Place cubes of chicken, chopped tomatoes and shredded lettuce in pita bread pockets, and pour in some of this sauce.

1 large cucumber
salt
1 scallion, chopped, including green part
1 tablespoon chopped parsley
1 tablespoon chopped dill
1 cup sour cream
freshly ground pepper to taste

Cut cucumber in half lengthwise and scoop out seeds; chop coarsely. Place in a strainer, sprinkle with salt and let stand 30 to 60 minutes. Press with the back of a spoon to drain completely, then remove any remaining moisture by drying cubes in paper towels.

Place cucumber cubes, scallion, parsley, dill and sour cream in a blender or food processor and pureé. Add salt and pepper to taste.

YIELD: ABOUT 2 CUPS OF SAUCE

PENNE WITH ASPARAGUS, GARDEN TOMATOES AND BRIE

Although the asparagus must be steamed, the rest of this sauce is uncooked, making it a perfect choice for a hot day. Put the Brie in the freezer briefly. This will make it much easier to trim the rind and cut the cheese into pieces. Once you combine the sauce and the pasta, serve this dish promptly. The flavors become too sharp if you let it stand too long.

1 pound asparagus
2¹/₂ pounds ripe tomatoes
1 pound Brie cheese
2 cloves garlic, crushed
¹/₄ cup freshly snipped parsley

1 cup extra-virgin olive oil
¹/₂ teaspoon salt
freshly ground pepper to taste
1 pound penne or similar pasta

Trim asparagus and cut diagonally into 2-inch pieces. Steam for 4 to 5 minutes until just barely tender. Reserve.

Cut tomatoes into small cubes and place in a large serving bowl. Remove rind from Brie and cut into similar-sized cubes. Add Brie, garlic, parsley, olive oil, salt, pepper and asparagus to bowl, mix gently, and set aside at room temperatures for about an hour to blend flavors.

Boil water for pasta, adding 1 tablespoon each of oil and salt. Cook penne according to package directions until al dente.

Drain and toss at once with asparagus-tomato sauce. Serve immediately.

YIELD: 6 SERVINGS

SADIE'S ALABAMA-STYLE GUMBO

3 slices bacon
1 medium onion, chopped
4 ears corn on the cob,
* uncooked*
1 large tomato

¹/₂ pound fresh okra (or 1
* 10-ounce box frozen okra,*
* thawed)*
salt and freshly ground pepper to
* taste*

Cook bacon until it is translucent and then drain and cut in pieces. To fat in pan, add onion and cook until tender.

Shuck corn and scrape the kernels off the cobs. There should be at least 2 cups. Add corn to frying pan and sauté for 5 to 10 minutes.

Peel tomato and slice thinly. Cut okra into small chunks. Add okra to corn mixture and lay tomato slices on top. Season with salt and pepper. Cover and cook slowly for about 25 to 30 minutes. Correct seasoning before serving.

YIELD: 6 SERVINGS

CELERY STIR-FRY WITH MIXED VEGETABLES

3 carrots
4 stalks celery
2 cups broccoli florets
2 tablespoons peanut oil
1 tablespoon sesame oil

1 large garlic clove, crushed
1 yellow pepper, chopped
2 tablespoons soy sauce
2 large scallions, including green part, chopped

You can make all manner of substitutions in this recipe. Just remember to add the slower-cooking vegetables first so that everything is evenly crisp-cooked at the end. And keep it colorful.

Peel the carrots and the tough outer strings of the celery. Trim the ends and cut each diagonally into ¼-inch slices.

Heat peanut oil in a wok or large frying pan until very hot. Add celery, carrots and broccoli, and stir-fry until vegetables begin to get tender, about 5 minutes. Add sesame oil, garlic and peppers, and stir-fry for 2 minutes more.

Add soy sauce and scallions, toss well and serve immediately.

YIELD: 4 SERVINGS

CORN-OFF-THE-COB WITH RED PEPPERS (AND OTHERS)

2 tablespoons butter or margarine
1 small onion, chopped
1 small red pepper, chopped
4 ears of corn, cooked

1 tablespoon chopped fresh basil
salt and freshly ground pepper to taste

Melt butter in a skillet and sauté onion until translucent. Add red pepper and cook until tender, about 5 minutes.

In the meantime, scrape kernels of corn off the cob—you should have about 2 cups.

Add corn and seasonings to onion-pepper mixture and cook for 2 or 3 minutes to blend flavors.

YIELD: 4 TO 6 SERVINGS

CUCUMBER SALAD MIZERIA

The title of this recipe—meaning, of course, "misery"—comes from the nickname earned by this traditional and inexpensive Polish salad when it was served too frequently in boarding schools during the numerous meatless holidays.

1 large cucumber, seedless if possible
salt
additional salt if needed
½ cup sour cream
1 teaspoon vinegar
2 teaspoons fresh lemon juice
1 teaspoon sugar
1 tablespoon finely chopped chives or white part of scallions
2–3 sprigs of dill leaves, finely snipped
freshly ground pepper to taste
optional: 1 hard-boiled egg, coarsely chopped

Peel cucumber. Slice thinly by hand or in a food processor. Place slices on a large flat dish, sprinkle with salt and cover with another plate, weighting it down with a heavy can or paperweight. Let stand 30 to 60 minutes. Drain off all the water.

Mix together sour cream, vinegar, lemon juice, sugar and chopped greens, and pour over cucumbers in a salad bowl. Correct seasoning, sprinkle with pepper and, if desired, with chopped egg. Keep refrigerated but serve within an hour to avoid too much water forming and diluting the dressing.

YIELD: 4 SERVINGS

There's little waste in celery: Seeds, stems and leaves can all be used—and not just for food. At one time, wild celery was used as smelling salts. In the Middle Ages, the plants served as laxatives and diuretics, to break up gall stones, to soothe swellings and wild beast bites. The Dutch gynecologist Van de Velde cited celery along with asparagus as an aphrodisiac.

DEEP-DISH RHUBARB PIE
WITH CINNAMON CRUST

Cinnamon sugar is a mixture of three parts sugar to one part cinnamon. Make enough so you can sprinkle it on your morning toast.

*1 3-ounce package cream
 cheese, at room temperature*
*1/3 cup butter or margarine, at
 room temperature*
3/4 cup flour
1 teaspoon cinnamon
1/2 teaspoon salt
*6 cups chopped rhubarb
 (about 2 pounds)*

1/2 cup flour
1 cup sugar
1/2 cup light corn syrup
1 tablespoon butter
cinnamon sugar
*optional: whipped cream or vanilla
 ice cream*

Preheat oven to 425°F.

Beat cream cheese and butter until fluffy. Add 3/4 cup flour, cinnamon and salt. Mix with a fork until well blended. Gather dough into a ball, wrap in wax paper and chill.

In the meantime, trim ends and leaves off rhubarb. Wash and pat dry. Cut into 1-inch pieces. Mix rhubarb and 1/2 cup flour in a 9-inch deep-dish pie plate or 9-inch square pan.

Bring sugar and corn syrup to a boil and pour over rhubarb. Dot with butter.

Remove pastry from refrigerator and, between 2 sheets of wax paper, roll out to 1 inch larger than the pan. Remove 1 sheet of wax paper and place dough over pie. Then peel off top sheet of paper. Fold under edges of dough and seal against side of pan. Cut several gashes in top of pie so steam can escape.

Place pie in oven on a cookie sheet to catch any overflow. Bake for 25 minutes. Serve warm, sprinkled with cinnamon sugar and, if you like, with whipped cream or vanilla ice cream.

YIELD: 8 SERVINGS

Rhubarb's name derives from the Greek rheon barbaron, or "coming from the banks of the Rha" (the Greek name for the Volga River), where barbarians first cultivated the pink-and-green stalks. The Latin rhabarbarum brought it closer to our own terminology. Early Americans dubbed it "pie plant" because of its affinity with pastry, but rhubarb is also delicious in meat stews or with fish.

RHUBARB BROWN BETTY

2 pounds fresh rhubarb
2 cups light brown sugar
1/2 cup flour

*4 tablespoons (1/2 stick) butter or
 margarine*

Preheat oven to 350°F.

Trim ends and leaves off rhubarb. Wash and pat dry. Cut into 1 1/2-inch pieces. Toss with 1 1/2 cups of the sugar in a heavy casserole. Cover tightly and bake for 20 minutes.

In the meantime, work together remaining sugar, flour and butter to form a crumbly topping. Remove casserole cover, spread topping over rhubarb, and bake 10 minutes more until topping has browned. Serve warm with heavy cream, whipped cream or vanilla ice cream.

YIELD: 4 TO 6 SERVINGS

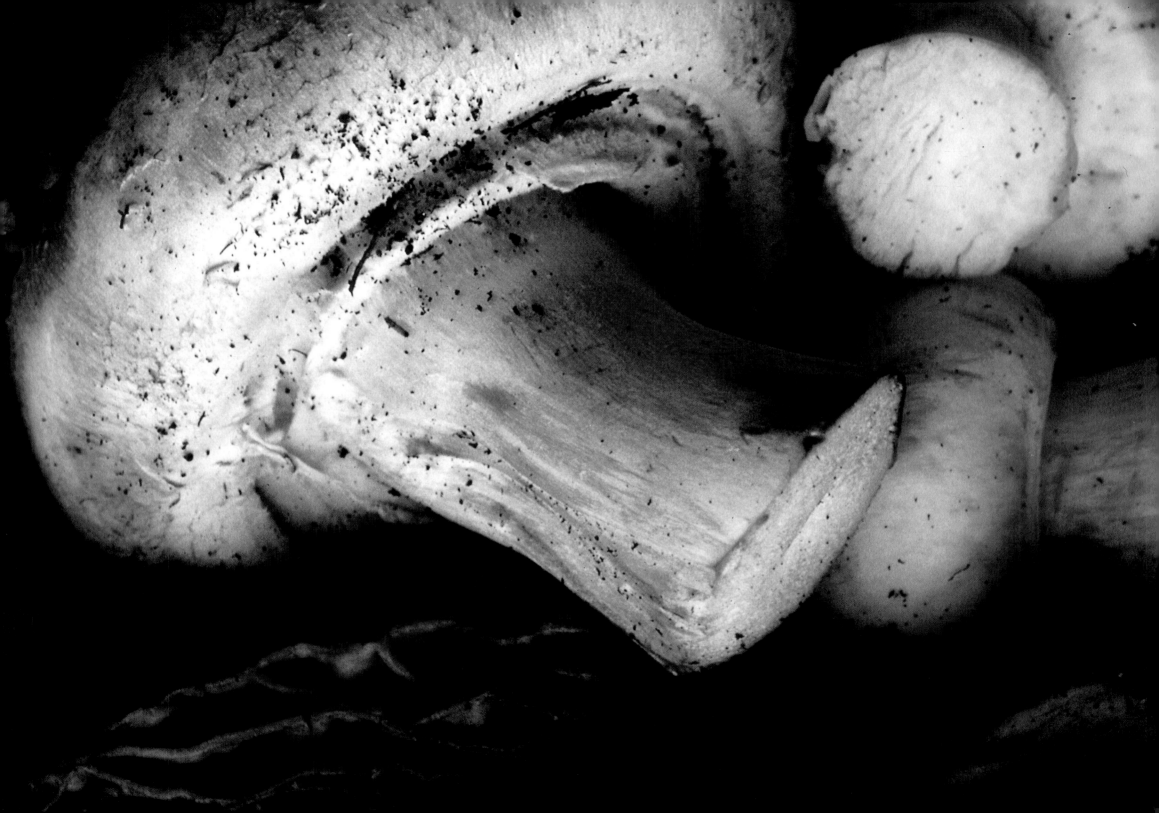

Mushrooms, Radishes, Avocados and Brussels Sprouts. Another group of unlikely bedfellows.

When the ancients saw mushrooms spring up overnight, they assumed they were created by divine lightning bolts. An aura of mystery and magic has followed these fungi, due in part to the hallucinogenic and poisonous properties of some of the wild varieties. The deadly toxins of mushrooms have done in many notables, from Russia's Alexander I and Pope Clement VII to the predecessor of Babar, King of the Elephants.

Happily, we now have expertly-trained others to do our foraging for us, and so we can enjoy a wide range of safe wild mushrooms, either fresh or dried, without going further than our local greenmarket or A&P. From shiitake and oyster mushrooms to chanterelles

SHORT THINGS

and cèpes to the extremely pricey morels, wild mushrooms are generally more flavorful than the bland common cultivated kind, which Florence Fabricant in *The New York Times* has called "the white bread of mushrooms." Bland or not, cultivated mushrooms are still the basis for some savory dishes. They should be purchased creamy-white, with thick and firm flesh.

The radish—always a bridesmaid, never a bride—is rarely the main reason for a dish. (If you've eaten cooked radishes, you'll understand why.) Eaten raw, this spicy little root adds a marvelous accent to many foods. Known to the Chinese and the Egyptians, the Greeks and the Romans—and believed to have been cultivated as early as the Neolithic era in Europe—radishes were highly esteemed in ancient times. In Athens, artisans made replicas of beets in silver and turnips in lead, but gold was reserved for the radish.

These peppery vegetables offer virtually no nourishment, but they are a dieter's delight: Four radishes equal a whopping five calories. They come in a surprising variety of colors and shapes: not only the familiar little red rat-tailed globe, but also the larger strongly favored black radish and the oblong white *daikon* of Japan that can reach giant (three-feet-long) proportions. Shop for smooth, firm, crisp radishes with a minimum of surface pits.

Avocados, which are not only short, but stout, are members of the laurel family. If the rhubarb is a vegetable eaten as a fruit, the avocado evens things out by being a fruit eaten as a vegetable. Ancient Aztecs left picture-writings of this fruit. They called it *ahuacatl,* short for *ahuacacuahatl,* or "testicle tree," which may account for its recurrent reputation as an aphrodisiac. There are two major types of avocado, the smooth and green-skinned winter fruit, and the summer fruit with the dark, pebbly skin that probably inspired its alternate name, alligator pear.

If left to ripen on the tree, avocados will fall to the ground and bruise, so they are picked early and must be held at room temperature to become ripe for eating. Since air causes discoloration of the exposed flesh, sprinkle cut avocado with a little lemon juice if you can't serve it right after peeling.

So you think you know the origin of Brussels sprouts? Wrong, or at least insofar as any proof exists. These little green rosettes are actually miniature head of cabbage and the source of this variety is still a mystery. Brussels sprouts grow in a most extraordinary fashion: encircling a thick, high stalk that grows straight up in the air, topped by an umbrella of cabbagy leaves that also shoot out intermittently along the stalk. The sprouts should be tightly furled and a healthy green color.

MUSHROOM KULEBIAKA

This a classic Russian savory pastry that is traditionally served with borscht or other hot soups.

1 cup flour
1 teaspoon baking powder
1/2 teaspoon salt
1/2 cup (1 stick) plus 3 tablespoons butter or margarine, at room temperature
4 ounces cream cheese, at room temperature

1 onion, finely chopped
1 pound mushrooms, sliced
1 cup cooked rice
3 tablespoons sour cream
1 teaspoon salt
freshly ground pepper to taste
1 hard-boiled egg, finely chopped
3 tablespoons freshly snipped dill
1 egg yolk, lightly beaten

Mix together flour, baking powder and salt. Cut the stick of butter and the cream cheese into pieces. Work into flour mixture with fingers or pastry blender until mixture resembles coarse meal. Form dough into a ball and chill at least 1 hour.

Sauté onion in the remaining 3 tablespoons of butter until translucent. Add mushrooms and cook until moisture has evaporated. Mix in all remaining ingredients except egg yolk and set aside to cool.

Preheat oven to 400°F.

Roll out dough into a rectangle about 10 x 14 inches 1/4-inch thick. Spread mushrooms filling in a sausage shape down the center length of the rectangle, leaving an inch uncovered at each end.

Lightly brush the edge of 1 side of the pastry with the beaten egg yolk. Fold the opposite side over so that it covers the filling. Fold the egg-coated side over that, to form a envelope. There should be about 1 1/2-inch overlap since the pastry will shrink in baking. Press gently to seal.

Pinch top and bottom ends closed. Brush with yolk and tuck snugly over the top of the filled cylinder. Carefully turn loaf seam-side down on a buttered baking sheet. Make light scores about 1 inch wide in the top of the loaf. Brush with beaten egg yolk.

Bake until golden brown, about 20 minutes. Slice to serve.

YIELD: 12 PORTIONS

BLACK RADISH PURÉE

The so-called Spanish or black radish is a big fellow, with a marvelous strong odor and more "bite" to the taste. It's favored by the Russians, who shred it finely, moisten it with salad oil, and serve it on black bread lightly spread with sweet butter.

Black radishes, with a flavor more pungent than that of their smaller red or white cousins, are better suited to cooking. You can serve this either as a side dish or as a spread with black bread to accompany a hearty winter soup.

3 black radishes (about 1 3/4 pounds)
salt to taste
1/2 cup heavy cream

1 medium potato
2 tablespoons melted butter or margarine
1 teaspoon dried chervil (or tarragon or basil)

Peel radishes and potato, cut in chunks, and cook in boiling salted water about 20 minutes, or until tender. Drain and place in blender with butter and cream; purée until smooth. Add seasonings.

YIELD: 6 SERVINGS

BRUSSELS SPROUTS SOUP

This creamy soup has a delicate tang to it—and not too many calories since the "cream" is buttermilk. You could also serve it chilled.

10 ounces Brussels sprouts (about 2 cups)	*3½ cups Chicken Broth (page 145)*
4 tablespoons (½ stick) butter or margarine	*salt and freshly ground pepper to taste*
1 cup chopped onions	*¾ cup buttermilk*
1 cup chopped, peeled potatoes	*chopped fresh chives for garnish*

Trim base of Brussels sprouts and remove any yellow or discolored leaves. Wash well, drain, cut sprouts into quarters and set aside.

In a medium-sized saucepan, melt butter and cook onion, stirring frequently, until transparent. Add potatoes and Brussels sprouts and sauté, stirring, for another minute or 2.

Add chicken broth, bring to a boil, and simmer, covered, for 20 minutes or until vegetables are completely tender. Purée in batches in a food processor or blender.

Add buttermilk and blend well. Season to taste with salt and pepper. When serving, add a sprinkle of chives to each portion.

YIELD: 4 TO 6 SERVINGS

CHUNKY GUACAMOLE SALAD

juice of 1 lemon (about 1½ tablespoons)	*½ teaspoon chili powder*
1 tablespoon vegetable oil	*2 ripe avocados*
1 large clove garlic, crushed	*2 ripe tomatoes*
½ teaspoon salt	*½ red onion, diced*

Combine lemon, oil, garlic, salt and chili powder to make a dressing; let stand.

Peel and cube avocados. Cut tomatoes in quarters and squeeze out seeds and juice. Cut pulp into cubes.

Combine avocados, tomatoes, and onion, and toss gently with dressing. Do not over-mix or salad will become mushy. Chill for an hour before serving on a bed of greens.

YIELD: 4 TO 6 SERVINGS

MEATBALLS IN GRAVY WITH BRUSSELS SPROUTS

Brussels sprouts, when overcooked, lose their color and can develop an unpleasantly strong flavor. It's best to steam them separately until barely tender and then add them to this dish. Or, if you have one, cook them in a microwave, where they will retain their bright green color.

1 pound ground beef	freshly ground pepper to taste
1/2 pound ground pork	1/3 cup flour
1 cup fresh bread crumbs	2 tablespoons butter or margarine
1/4 cup milk	2 cups beef broth
1 egg	1/2 cup sour cream
1 small onion, minced	11/2 pounds Brussels sprouts
1 tablespoon Worcestershire sauce	12 ounces extra-wide egg noodles
11/2 teaspoons salt	

Mix together beef, pork, bread crumbs, milk, egg, onion, Worcestershire sauce, salt and pepper. Form into balls about the same size as the Brussels sprouts. Roll the meatballs in the flour to coat them. Reserve the leftover flour.

Heat the butter in a large frying pan and brown the meatballs on all sides. Remove them with a slotted spoon. Whisk 3 tablespoons of the reserved flour into the pan drippings. Cook over medium heat for a minute or 2. Whisk in beef broth and cook until it bubbles and thickens; then whisk in the sour cream.

Return meatballs to pan, cover and simmer for 10 minutes so meatballs are cooked through.

In the meantime, trim base of Brussels sprouts and remove any yellowed or damaged leaves. Cut an "X" in each base. Steam until tender, about 10 minutes for medium-sized sprouts. Do not overcook.

Cook noodles according to package directions. Drain.

Add cooked sprouts to meatballs and gravy. Correct seasoning if necessary. Serve over noodles.

YIELD: 6 SERVINGS

MUSHROOM, LEEK AND SAUSAGE PIE

1 9-inch partially prebaked pastry shell made with Basic Pie Pastry (page 148)	3/4 pound mushrooms, sliced
	3 eggs, lightly beaten
2 large leeks	3/4 cup half-and-half
4 tablespoons (1/2 stick) butter or margarine	1 teaspoon salt
	freshly ground pepper to taste
	1/2 pound kielbasa, thinly sliced

Cut roots and tops off the leeks, leaving 2 inches of leaves. Wash thoroughly, cut into rings, and rinse again. Drain well. Sauté leeks in butter for about 5 minutes, then add mushrooms and cook until soft, about 5 minutes more.

Combine eggs, half-and-half, salt and pepper.

Preheat oven to 350°F.

Arrange leeks, mushrooms and sliced kielbasa evenly in partially prebaked pastry shell. Pour egg mixture over all. Bake for 30 minutes or until set. Cool slightly before serving.

YIELD: 6 SERVINGS

BONELESS CHICKEN BREASTS WITH WILD MUSHROOMS AND BALSAMIC VINEGAR

The flavor of boletus mushrooms (porcini, cèpes, et cetera) intensifies in the dried state, so half an ounce goes a long way—and is just about what most of us can afford.

1/2 ounce dried porcini	2 to 3 tablespoons butter or margarine
4 ounces fresh shiitake mushrooms	salt and freshly ground pepper to taste
12 ounces cultivated white mushrooms	2 cloves garlic, minced
6 whole chicken breasts	1 cup Chicken Broth (page 145)
1/2 cup flour	6 tablespoons balsamic vinegar
2 to 3 tablespoons olive oil	1 bay leaf

Soak dried mushrooms in warm water to cover until soft, about 1/2 hour. Drain, reserving a few tablespoons of the water. Pick over mushrooms to remove any remaining grit, and chop. Rinse the shiitake and white mushrooms, pat dry and set aside.

Cut each chicken breast in half lengthwise and trim off any fat and membranes. Place flour in a plastic bag and shake chicken pieces, 2 at a time, to coat. Shake off excess.

In a large, heavy frying pan, heat 1 tablespoon of the oil and 1 tablespoon of the butter. Place half the chicken breasts in pan and sprinkle with salt and pepper. Cook over moderately high heat for about 3 minutes until golden brown on one side. Turn, sprinkling other side with salt and pepper and cook until second side has browned. Remove from pan, add 1 more tablespoon each of oil and butter, and repeat procedure with remaining six breast pieces. Remove from pan.

If necessary, add remaining tablespoon of oil and butter to skillet with the garlic. Add the shiitake and cultivated mushrooms and cook until they begin to yield their juices. Add dried mushrooms. Pour in chicken stock, bring to a boil, and stir to loosen any browned particles on the bottom of the pan. Add 5 tablespoons of the vinegar and the bay leaf, and return the chicken pieces to the pan.

Cover well and simmer for about 10 minutes, until breasts are just cooked through, turning pieces occasionally. If sauce is still thin, remove chicken pieces to a warm platter, cover with aluminum foil, and let sauce with mushrooms cook uncovered for another 5 minutes or so to reduce.

Remove bay leaf, add remaining tablespoon of vinegar to pan, and correct seasoning if necessary. Pour sauce and mushrooms over the chicken and serve.

YIELD: 6 TO 8 AMPLE SERVINGS

Until modern cultivation took the mystery out of mushrooms, it was hard to tell the safe varieties from the deadly ones. It is said that when the Emperor Claudius died of poisonous mushrooms administered by his fourth wife, Agrippina, Rome's chief source of grief was its inability to determine, for its citizens' self-preservation, just which variety did him in.

PASTA SALAD WITH AVOCADOS, TOMATOES AND SMOKED TURKEY

The avocado dressing for this salad is also good on sliced beefsteak tomatoes and cold cooked shrimp or other seafood.

2 very ripe, small avocados
1 clove garlic, roughly chopped
1/4 cup Herb Vinaigrette
 (page 145)
1 tablespoon fresh lemon juice
8 ounces spiral noodles

1 1/2 cups cubed ripe tomato
1/2 pound smoked turkey, cubed
 (about 1 1/2 cups)
salt and freshly ground pepper to
 taste

Cut one of the avocados in half and remove the seed. Spoon out flesh into blender or food processor. Add garlic and purée until smooth.

Add vinaigrette and lemon juice and mix well. Chill for 30 minutes to blend flavors.

Cook noodles according to package directions and drain. Run pasta under cool water, drain again and let cool.

Peel second avocado. Cut in half, remove the seed and cut flesh into cubes. In a serving bowl, mix pasta, tomatoes, avocado cubes and turkey and toss with avocado dressing. Season to taste.

YIELD: 4 SERVINGS

SWORDFISH STEAKS WITH RADISH-CUCUMBER GARNISH

The cooking time for swordfish will vary according to the thickness of the steaks. Fish should be moist when it is served. The rule of eight to ten minutes' broiling time per inch of thickness is a pretty good gauge.

1/4 pound radishes
1 cucumber
1/2 teaspoon salt
large handful fresh dill, snipped
3 tablespoons Mayonnaise
 (pages 145–46)

3 tablespoons sour cream
salt and freshly ground pepper to
 taste
2 pounds swordfish steaks

Trim and wash radishes and slice thinly—you should have about 1 cup.

Peel cucumber, slice in half lengthwise and scoop out seeds. Slice thinly. Toss in a strainer with 1/2 teaspoon salt. Let stand for 30 minutes to yield up moisture. Squeeze out excess.

Combine radishes, cucumber, dill, mayonnaise and sour cream in a small bowl and toss to blend well. Season to taste. Chill.

Preheat broiler and pan. Season swordfish steaks to taste. Broil about 4 inches from the flame, turning once. Top each steak with a portion of radish-cucumber garnish.

YIELD: 4 TO 6 SERVINGS

Artichokes, Jerusalem Artichokes, Ginger, Horse-radish, Celeriac, Fennel and Kohlrabi. These are the oddballs of the vegetable world, by virtue of their shape or flavor the anomalies in their botanical families. Weirdly shaped or misshapen, gnarled or spiky, blessed with distinctive flavor but offputting in appearance—all, that is, save the sleek plump fennel, which stands out as the beauty among the beasts but is no less strange.

The amazing thing about the artichoke is that anyone ever braved its sharp points and thistle to discover it was edible. The award for culinary valor evidently goes to an Arab, since its first recorded name, *al-kharshuf*, is an Arabic one. "Four-footed beasts instinc-

ECCENTRICS

tively refuse to touch them," wrote Pliny, and yet they fetched the highest prices in the vegetable markets of Rome and became the passion of Catherine de Medici. Jan Grigson calls them "the vegetable expression of civilized living" and shows no surprise that they were once regarded as an aphrodisiac, an association that is only enhanced by the knowledge that Henry VIII was very fond of them. When buying artichokes, pick firm, solid heads with compact green leaves and no brown spots. Size does not determine maturity or quality.

Jerusalem artichokes have nothing to do with either Jerusalem or artichokes, outside of a slight similarity in cooked flavor. The "Jeru-salem" is probably a corruption of the Italian *girasole*, or sunflower,

the plant family to which this tuber belongs. Though it originated in North America, it has never been accorded the popularity that its delicate, nutlike flavor merits. However, the Jerusalem artichoke was a mainstay of early colonial survival, affording a nutritious food during the "six weeks' want" between the exhaustion of winter food supplies and the first harvests.

Ginger and horseradish aren't much to look at, poor things, but they make up for their grubby appearance with a marvelous pungency. Too strong to be eaten alone, they are prized for the flavor they add to other foods. The so-called ginger "root" is actually an underground stem, or rhizome. (True roots don't produce buds or nodes; rhizomes do.) Native to tropical Asia, ginger followed the trade routes to ancient Rome. There it cost ten times as much as black pepper because the Roman government, knowing a fertile source of taxation when it saw one, figured its great popularity could withstand high import levies. Waverley Root quotes an unidentified Dr. Fallet as saying that ginger "confers on those who use it absolute power over any tigers they may happen to meet." Most of us are content to use its strength to heat up our cooking. Ginger is available fresh, preserved or crystallized.

Horseradish *is* a true root, undoubtedly the most pungent of all the edible roots. A *Gourmet* article by Lillian Langseth-Christensen described the pleasure of its bite: "a simple dinner" that "can be turned into a tear fest" with the addition of freshly grated horseradish to roast beef; or "an innocent-appearing applesauce that sends the unsuspecting guest right up through the dining-room ceiling." Horseradish probably originated in central Europe where, in any case, the Germans mastered its use in a variety of sauces and cleared their sinuses in the process.

Imagine celery with its root blown up large and its stalks shrunk down, and you'll have celeriac, also called celery root. Waverley

Root tells us that it was "developed in Renaissance times by garden-ers who persuaded celery to become a turnip." Its convoluted and fibrous skin, hardly enticing to the eye, hides a white interior that has been accurately described as having great character.

All the root vegetables described in this section should be pur-chased when young and firm; choose those that are least bumpy and twisted so that peeling is less of a chore. Both celeriac and Jerusalem artichokes must be dropped into lemon juice and water after slicing to prevent discoloration.

Fennel, a.k.a. "anise" or the Italian "finocchio," has ribs that are striated like celery and leaves that resemble dill, both relatives in the parsley family. Its aniselike flavor, of course, is completely different. Fennel was widely known in ancient Greece and an area where it grew profusely was called "Marathon" after the Greek name for this vegetable. There are actually two kinds: herb fennel, a feathery dill-like herb used to flavor fish; and the bulbous vegetable that often serves the same purpose and is more commonly found in markets. Fennel has fewer calories than almost any other vegetable (and thus, of course, less nutritive value). Look for fresh green leaves and crisp, greenish-white bulbs.

And now for something completely different: kohlrabi, a globe with leaf stems jutting out in all directions that looks as if it had just flown in from outer space. Its Germanic name, which literally translates as cabbage-turnip, suggests a strange alliance, but it's a turnip in shape only and is really a cardcarrying member of the cabbage clan. The edible part of this vegetable is not a root but, like fennel, a swelling of the stem right above the ground. Purchase medium-sized spheres that are as smooth skinned as possible; the leaves can be cooked separately like kale or Swiss chard and should be young and green.

CHILLED ARTICHOKES WITH SHRIMP MAYONNAISE

6 artichokes
salt
2 tablespoons lemon juice
1 pound shrimp, shelled and
   deveined
1¼ cups Mayonnaise (page 145)

¼ cup lemon juice
2 teaspoons minced fresh
   tarragon, or ½ teaspoon dried
freshly ground pepper to taste
1 tablespoon capers

Wash artichokes under cold running water. Cut off stems at base and remove small bottom leaves. Slice off about 1 inch from top of artichokes and trim the remaining points off the leaves with scissors.

Drop prepared artichokes into a large pot containing 7 to 8 quarts of boiling salted water, and add 2 tablespoons of lemon juice to prevent the leaves from discoloring. Cover and boil gently 30 to 45 minutes, depending upon size, until bottoms can be pierced easily with a fork. Drain well upside down on a rack.

When artichokes are cool enough to handle, gently spread the leaves and remove the choke (thistle portion) by pulling out the light-colored innermost cone of leaves in one piece and scraping away the central fuzzy portion with a spoon. Set aside.

Boil 2 cups of water in a pot large enough to hold the shrimp. Add a pinch of salt. Cook shrimp for about 3 minutes, until they turn pink. Reserve ½ cup of the cooking water and drain.

Place the mayonnaise in a blender. Add shrimp, reserved water, ¼ cup lemon juice, 1 teaspoon salt, tarragon and pepper. Blend only until shrimp are slightly broken up. Stir in capers and chill (mixture will thicken in the refrigerator).

When ready to serve, fill the artichoke cavities with equal amounts of the shrimp mayonnaise.

YIELD: 6 SERVINGS (ABOUT 2½ CUPS OF SHRIMP MAYONNAISE)

SCALLOP TOAST

This is an interesting twist on the traditional Chinese shrimp toast. If you do not have stale bread, you can leave the individual slices out on the counter for a few hours turning slices so both sides dry out; or place slices on a cookie sheet in a 250°F. oven for about five minutes on each side. Dry slices absorb far less oil than fresh ones.

1 pound fresh bay scallops
1 cup chopped scallions,
   including green parts
4 thin slices peeled fresh ginger
½ teaspoon sugar
1 egg
1 tablespoon cornstarch

1 teaspoon salt
1 tablespoon dry sherry
½ teaspoon sesame oil
freshly ground pepper to taste
10 to 12 thin slices stale white
   bread
peanut oil for deep frying

Place all ingredients except bread and peanut oil in a food processor and process until cohesive but not puréed. Spread mixture thickly on 1 side of each slice of bread.

Heat oil in a large frying pan to 375°F. Working with 4 slices at a time, fry slices, scallop side down, until topping turns golden brown. Turn and fry briefly until golden on the other side. Remove and drain thoroughly on paper towels. Cut each slice into 4 diamonds and serve with duck sauce and Chinese mustard. Toast may be kept hot in the oven if you cannot serve it immediately.

YIELD: 40 TO 48 PIECES

CECELE FRAENKEL'S
OYSTER-ARTICHOKE RAMEKINS

Okay, you're absolutely right. This is a lot of trouble. But if you love fresh artichokes and oysters, you may agree that it's worth the fuss. One advantage is that you won't have to bother trimming the artichokes as you do for the previous recipe since you'll be dismembering them as soon as they are cooked.

3 artichokes	1 teaspoon salt
3/4 teaspoon salt	1 teaspoon white pepper
1 tablespoon lemon juice	Tabasco sauce to taste
3 tablespoons butter or margarine	1 teaspoon Worcestershire sauce
1 1/2 tablespoons flour	2 tablespoons dry sherry
1/2 cup milk	1 tablespoon chopped pimento
1/4 cup heavy cream	3/4 cup freshly made bread crumbs
1 pint (about 2 dozen) shelled oysters and liquid	1 tablespoon butter or margarine

Boil enough water to cover the artichokes and add salt and lemon juice. Cover and boil gently for 30 to 45 minutes, until bottoms can be pierced easily with a fork. Drain well. Remove artichoke leaves and set aside. Remove and discard the choke (thistle portion) to expose the smooth bottoms, or hearts. Scrape the flesh off the leaves into a small bowl. Cut artichoke hearts into small cubes and add to bowl.

Preheat oven to 450°F.

In a heavy saucepan, melt butter and flour and cook over moderate heat for 2 minutes without browning. Pour milk and cream into saucepan, stirring until mixture simmers, thickens, and becomes smooth.

Drain oyster liquid into saucepan and stir to blend. Heat oysters in a separate pan until excess liquid has evaporated; add to cream sauce and simmer 5 minutes. Add salt, pepper, Tabasco, Worcestershire, sherry, pimento and artichoke cubes.

Pour into 4 buttered 4-inch ramekins, top with crumbs, and dot with butter. Bake for 6 to 7 minutes, until crumbs start to brown.

YIELD: 4 SERVINGS

Jerusalem artichokes are the only vegetable with a sliding calorie count. When first harvested, their carbohydrates take the form of inulin, a hard-to-digest sugar that causes "windiness" and has few calories. As they are stored, the inulin converts to two absorbable sugars—glucose and fructose—and the dieter pays the price. Depending upon age, a hundred grams of Jerusalem artichokes (about three ounces) can range from seven to seventy-five calories.

SOUR CREAM AND HORSERADISH SAUCE

If you thought onions made you weep, wait until you work with fresh horseradish. Don't even think about grating horseradish by hand; use a blender or food processor, and keep the cover on until it's absolutely necessary to take it off! This sauce is delicious with roast beef, pot roast and baked potatoes. You can even bake potatoes, mash the insides with this sauce, and stuff the mixture back into the shells for a piquant side dish.

To grate fresh horseradish, peel a section, cut it off and wash well to remove any traces of dirt. Cut into pieces. Blend or process them as finely as possible.

1 cup sour cream	1 tablespoon sugar, preferably
3 tablespoons freshly grated	superfine
horseradish	1/2 teaspoon salt
3 tablespoons white vinegar	freshly ground pepper to taste

Empty sour cream into a small bowl. Add horseradish, vinegar, sugar, salt and pepper and mix well. Let stand for at least 1 hour so that flavors will blend well. If not serving right away, chill. If you are serving this sauce with hot food, take it out of the refrigerator about an hour before serving so it loses its chill.

YIELD: ABOUT 1 1/2 CUPS SAUCE

JERUSALEM ARTICHOKE SOUP

1 pound Jerusalem artichokes	1/2 cup heavy cream
4 tablespoons (1/2 stick) butter or	3/4 teaspoon salt
margarine	freshly ground pepper to taste
1 medium onion, sliced	watercress for garnish
5 cups Chicken Broth (page 145)	

Scrub and peel the Jerusalem artichokes and cut into chunks.

Melt butter and sauté artichokes and onion for about 5 minutes. Add chicken broth and simmer for about 1/2 hour, or until vegetables are tender.

Using food processor or blender, purée the soup. Return to the pot, add cream, and season. Bring to serving temperature and garnish with chopped watercress.

YIELD: 6 SERVINGS

STIR-FRIED SHREDDED KOHLRABI, CARROTS AND PEPPERS

Choose medium-sized kohlrabies (yes, that plural is correct). The tiny ones are a nuisance to peel, and the largest ones can be woody and bitter. Jane Grigson describes the ideal as "between a golf ball and tennis ball in size." If you don't have thyme you can substitute basil or oregano in this dish.

1½ pounds kohlrabi (without the leaves)
3 carrots, peeled and coarsely grated
½ large red pepper, diced
4 tablespoons (½ stick) butter or margarine

1 tablespoon freshly snipped thyme
½ tablespoon freshly snipped parsley
salt and freshly ground pepper to taste

Strip stems from kohlrabies and peel them thoroughly. If you're going to grate them by hand, leave some of the woody tip to hold on to. Grate coarsely by hand or in the food processor. Toss with carrot and red pepper.

In a large skillet, melt butter. When it sizzles, add vegetables and stir-fry for 5 or 6 minutes, until vegetables start to get tender but still retain their crispness.

Add thyme, parsley, salt and pepper. Toss well.

YIELD: 6 SERVINGS

GINGER SHRIMP IN BEER BATTER

1 pound large fresh shrimp
1 12-ounce can beer
1 tablespoon minced fresh ginger
1 teaspoon minced garlic
2 tablespoons chopped parsley

1½ teaspoons salt
¾ cup flour
¼ teaspoon baking powder
vegetable oil for deep frying

Shell and devein shrimp but leave the tails on.

Combine 6 ounces of the beer, ginger, garlic, parsley and ½ teaspoon of the salt. Marinate shrimp in this mixture for 4 hours in the refrigerator.

One hour before frying, mix remaining beer with flour, remaining teaspoon of salt and baking powder. Beat with wire whisk until smooth and let stand at room temperature for 1 hour.

Heat oil in a skillet or deep-fat fryer to 375°F. Dry shrimp thoroughly with paper towels, dip into beer batter and fry 2 or 3 at a time in hot oil until nicely browned. Drain on absorbent paper.

YIELD: 3 to 4 SERVINGS

FENNEL SAUTÉED IN BLACK BUTTER

If the outer layer of the fennel bulb is tough and stringy, cut away that section—but then you must allow one head per person.

2 large or 4 small bulbs of fennel	grated rind and juice of one lemon
5 tablespoons butter or margarine	1 tablespoon chopped parsley
salt and freshly ground pepper	1/2 teaspoon oregano
to taste	1/2 teaspoon basil

Wash fennel, trim stalks and base and cut in thick slices.

Melt 3 tablespoons of the butter in a large skillet, add fennel slices and sprinkle with salt and pepper. Cover and cook slowly, stirring occasionally, for 5 minutes or until fennel is just tender. Uncover pan and cook over high heat for a few minutes more to let moisture evaporate—but do not let fennel get mushy. Transfer to a warm serving dish.

Add remaining butter to pan and cook until it turns golden brown (not black). Quickly add lemon rind and juice and the herbs. Pour the butter sauce over the fennel while it is still foaming and serve at once.

YIELD: 4 SERVINGS

ARTICHOKE PURÉE

More trouble. Remember, life is a trade-off. If you want to make this ahead of time, you can keep it hot by placing the pot in a frying pan containing hot water. Or you can let it cool and reheat it in a microwave (in a microwaveable dish, of course). Don't bother snipping off the points of the leaves for this recipe.

3 large or 4 medium artichokes	pinch of dried thyme
1 teaspoon salt	salt and freshly ground pepper to taste
1 tablespoon lemon juice	1/4 teaspoon nutmeg
2 medium potatoes, peeled and sliced	2 tablespoons butter or margarine
1 tablespoon heavy cream optional	chopped parsley or chives for garnish

Boil enough water to cover the artichokes and add salt and lemon juice. Cover and boil gently for 30 to 45 minutes, until bottoms can be pierced easily with a fork. Drain well.

While artichokes are cooking, boil potatoes in a separate pot until tender. Drain and place in bowl of food processor.

Remove artichoke leaves and discard the choke (thistle portion) to expose the smooth bottoms or hearts. Scrape the flesh off the leaves into bowl of food processor and add cubed artichoke hearts.

To vegetables in food processor add butter, nutmeg, thyme, salt and pepper. Process until smooth. If purée seems too thick, add the cream. Just before serving, sprinkle on parsley or chives.

YIELD: 4 SERVINGS

Fennel's curves recall a plump odalisque painted by Ingres, and the bulb without its leaves has a configuration not unlike the human heart. "Above the lowly plants it towers," wrote Longfellow of this vegetable. "And in an earlier age than ours/Was gifted with the wondrous powers/Lost vision to restore." When cooked, fennel loses much of its anise flavor and becomes sweeter.

GINGERSNAPS-FROM-SCRATCH

Fresh ginger dries out easily—but if you store it in a tightly closed plastic bag in the refrigerator, its natural moisture may cause it to get moldy. Put a paper towel in the plastic bag to absorb the moisture, and the ginger will keep for several weeks. If you want to keep it longer, peel the ginger and cut it into pieces that will fit into a small jar. Cover them with dry sherry or, better yet, vodka, which will not alter the taste of the ginger and will preserve it indefinitely.

What gives these gingersnaps their depth of flavor is fresh ginger, rather than the ground spice. If you have a food processor, they are really easy to make. Try them with Peach Sorbet (page 117) or Cinnamon-Scented Persimmon Whip (page 126). If you can find confectionery pearl sugar in a specialty food store during the winter holiday season, you can dip the dough in these white crystals before baking, for a snowy effect. Plan ahead so that you can chill this dough for two hours before baking.

2¼ cups unbleached presifted
  flour
1½ teaspoons baking soda
1 teaspoon cinnamon
½ teaspoon ground cloves
½ teaspoon nutmeg
1 1-inch cube of peeled fresh
  ginger

¾ cup (1½ sticks) butter or
  margarine
1 egg
¼ cup molasses
1 cup packed brown sugar

In a food processor, mix together flour, baking soda, cinnamon, cloves and nutmeg by pulsing on and off several times. Remove from processor and set aside.

With the processor running, drop the cube of ginger through the feed tube and process for a few seconds until minced. Add butter and pulse on and off 6 or 7 times until blended. Add egg, molasses and sugar and process for 30 seconds, stopping occasionally to scrape down the bowl. Add flour mixture and pulse on and off about 5 times or just until flour disappears.

Chill the dough in plastic wrap for at least 2 hours.

Preheat oven to 350°F.

Form the dough by hand into 1-inch balls. Place 2 inches apart on lightly greased baking sheets. Bake 10 to 12 minutes or until cookies are firm but still soft. They will harden as they cool.

YIELD: ABOUT 50 COOKIES

WILLIAM PROOPS'S CELERIAC-APPLE PURÉE

The amount of heavy cream you use in this recipe will depend on whether you like your purées firm or loose. If you're watching calories, you can substitute Chicken Broth (page 145) or consommé for the cream. You can easily double this recipe for Thanksgiving dinner or any large crowd.

1½ pounds celeriac
juice of ½ lemon
1 pound tart-sweet apples such as
  Cortland or Ida Red, peeled,
  cored and quartered
2 tablespoons butter or margarine

⅓ to ½ cup heavy cream (to
  taste)
salt and white pepper to taste
pinch of nutmeg
fresh parsley or chives for garnish

Slice bumpy ends off celery roots (celeriac), peel them and cut into large chunks. Drop into a bowl of water mixed with lemon juice as you go to prevent discoloration.

Boil enough water to cover celery roots and apples, and cook *celery roots only* for about 15 minutes, or until almost tender. Add apples and cook for 3 to 5 minutes more, until both are very tender. Drain well.

Transfer in batches to a blender or food processor and purée, adding butter and enough cream to make mixture silky. Season with salt, white pepper and nutmeg. Garnish with chopped parsley or chives.

YIELD: 4 TO 6 SERVINGS

From beds and brambles, bushes and bogs, berries are gathered all over America. In New England the season begins with strawberries in June and ends with cranberries in November. In between are some fine months of picking raspberries, blackberries and blueberries. The price is scratched arms, stained fingers and snagged clothing, but what a prize!

Raspberries have been traced back to Mesolithic sites in Denmark and Neolithic sites in Switzerland, though most botanists think they originated in Asia. Both Moses' burning bush and Christ's crown of thorns were probably blackberry brambles. The modern strawberry was born in 1714, when the large lush Chilean strawberry, tasting a bit of pineapple, was crossed with the scarlet Virginia meadow strawberry.

BERRIES & CHERRIES

Strawberries are one of the few fruits whose seeds are on the outside. There are several theories as to how they got their name: because their seeds resemble straw; because straw was used as a covering for the berry beds to discourage weeds; and because strawberry runners "stray" away from the plant. Strawberries yield more food per acre in a shorter time than any other fruit. "Wee can not sett down foote but tred on strawberries," wrote one of the first English visitors to Maryland. Perhaps the abundance of strawberries, wherever they grow, explains why a certain Mme. Tallien, during the reign of Napoleon, felt she could indulge herself by adding strawberry juice to her bath as a skin softener. It took twenty-two pounds of the berries, crushed, every time she bathed.

Raspberries, blackberries and strawberries are highly perishable. Whether you pick them or find them in the market, try to capture that peak moment of ripeness and avoid soft spots and any mold. If these berries must be washed, do it quickly, just before using.

Blueberries and cranberries are indigenous to North America. There is some confusion about the difference between huckleberries and blueberries. The answer? Huckleberries have large, hard, bony seeds. The North American Blueberry Council maintains that if Mark Twain had known what grew along the banks of the Mississippi and Ohio rivers, he would have called Tom Sawyer's buddy Blueberry Finn. Good blueberries should be plump and firm, with a dark color and silvery bloom.

Cranberries, like blueberries, belong to the heather family and were important in the Indian diet. Since their pink blossoms resemble the head of a crane, the Pilgrims christened them "crane berries." Their natural acidity enables cranberries to keep almost indefinitely. In order to reach the marketplace, cranberries must pass the unique "bounce test": Each berry is given seven chances to bounce over four-inch barriers and only the lively ones go on to market.

Cherries were first cultivated by the Babylonians and Assyrians and they figure in early writings from Greece and Rome, China and Japan. American cherries come largely from the Pacific Northwest and are of two principal varieties: sweet and sour, the latter used primarily for cooking. Cherry skins can range from dark purple-red to almost white or yellow, and their meat from white to dark red. Choose them one by one, looking for bright and glossy fruit with flexible green stems.

Cranberries are a native American fruit, used by the Indians (and later the Pilgrims) not only for food but also to treat arrow wounds and to dye fabrics. Cranberries were picked by hand until wooden-fingered scoops were devised, but modern technology has replace these with less picturesque mechanical pickers.

HUNGARIAN CHERRY SOUP

This is, of course, a summer soup—not too sweet and, without the cream, not too rich.

4 cups ripe, red or black sweet
  cherries, stemmed
¼ cup sugar, approximately
juice of 1 lemon
2 tablespoons cornstarch
¼ cup cold water
optional: ½ cup heavy cream

½ cup red wine
½ lemon, seeded and thinly
  sliced
1 2-inch stick cinnamon

Place cherries in a large pot with 1 cup of water, wine, lemon slices, cinnamon stick and sugar. Bring to a boil and simmer for 15 minutes.

Press through a sieve, discarding lemon pieces, cherry pits and cinnamon.

Add enough water to make 1 quart. Return the mixture to the pot. Add lemon juice and bring to a boil.

Make a smooth paste of the cornstarch and ¼ cup cold water and add to the simmering soup. Stir until thickened. Taste, and add more sugar if desired.

Remove from heat and chill.

Just before serving, whip the cream and serve soup in cold soup bowls with a spoonful of whipped cream in each serving.

YIELD: 6 SERVINGS

SUE SIEGLER'S RUBY RELISH
(CRANBERRIES, RASPBERRIES, ORANGES AND WALNUTS)

1 cup water
1 cup sugar
1 12-ounce package cranberries
½ pint fresh raspberries, or 1 cup
  frozen unsweetened
  raspberries

2 large or 3 small navel oranges
1 teaspoon vanilla
½ cup whole shelled walnuts or
  pecans

Heat water and sugar until sugar dissolves. Pick over cranberries and discard any unripe or blemished ones. Add cranberries to pot and bring to a boil; continue cooking for 2 or 3 minutes until the skins begin to burst and the juice thickens. Add raspberries and cook for a minute or 2 more. Remove from heat.

Cut unpeeled oranges in half from navel to stem, then horizontally into thirds. Slice each segment away from the peel and remove all membranes. (If you prefer smaller segments, you can cut these in half.) Add oranges and vanilla to cranberry and raspberry mixture. Cool. (If you are not planning to serve this right away, you can freeze it.)

Add the walnuts just before serving. They will get soggy if they remain in the relish too long.

YIELD: ABOUT 4 CUPS

BRAISED VEAL WITH CHERRIES

1½ cups fresh sweet cherries, stemmed
¾ cup sugar
1 4- to 5-pound veal rump
¼ cup oil
1 small onion, chopped
1 cup slivered cooked ham

1 teaspoon salt
⅛ teaspoon freshly ground pepper
¼ teaspoon ground cloves
juice of 1 lemon
2 tablespoons flour

Combine cherries with sugar and 2 cups of water in a small saucepan. Bring to a boil, then reduce heat and simmer for 5 minutes. Drain cherries, reserving the liquid. Cool slightly and carefully remove pits.

In a large, heavy-bottomed pan, brown veal slowly on all sides in oil. Add onion and ham and brown lightly. Add seasonings, 1 cup of reserved poaching liquid, and lemon juice. Cover tightly and simmer for 2 hours, or until meat is tender.

Remove meat and keep warm.

Combine flour with ¼ cup water until smooth. Stir into pan liquid and cook, stirring, until smooth and thick. Add cherries and heat. Pour sauce over sliced roast and serve with rice.

YIELD: 4 TO 6 SERVINGS

DOUG'S TROPICAL COOLER

In our high-tech culinary world, food processors have replaced blenders in many households, but a blender is really preferable to get the smooth consistency that's ideal for this drink.

ice cubes
½ pint strawberries, hulled and sliced
¼ fresh pineapple, cored and cut into chunks

1 banana, sliced
3 tablespoons sugar
⅓ cup water

Fill a 5- to 6-cup blender about halfway with ice cubes. Add remainder of ingredients in the order listed. Blend on high until completely liquefied and frothy.

This drink is best if served immediately, but you can store it in the freezer for a short time.

YIELD: 1 QUART

TWO SAUCES FOR FRESH BERRIES

Ripe berries are best eaten just as they are—and quickly, since they don't keep well. But a good sauce can't hurt. These sauces work well with any berries—and with peaches, plums, pears and even fruits with other initial letters. The Crème Fraîche will keep up to several weeks in the refrigerator.

Crème Fraîche

½ pint (1 cup) sour cream   brown sugar
1 pint heavy cream

Mix creams together and heat gently to a temperature of no more than 85 to 90°F. Pour into a container, cover loosely and leave at room temperature in a warm place for 6 to 8 hours or overnight or until cream has thickened. Stir, cover and refrigerate. Serve with berries and brown sugar.

YIELD: 3 CUPS

Light Almond Custard

4 egg yolks   1¾ cups milk
½ cup sugar   1 tablespoon vanilla
1 teaspoon cornstarch   ½ teaspoon almond extract

Beat egg yolks and sugar in large bowl of electric mixer until mixture becomes light yellow and very thick. Beat in the cornstarch.

Heat milk to boiling and add to yolk mixture in a thin stream, beating constantly to incorporate. Pour into a heavy-bottomed saucepan and cook, stirring constantly, over moderate heat until custard thickens enough to coat the spoon. Remove from heat and strain. Add extracts and mix well. Chill.

YIELD: ABOUT 2 CUPS

CRÈME BRÛLÉE WITH RASPBERRIES

2 cups fresh raspberries   1 teaspoon cornstarch
⅓ cup granulated sugar   2½ cups heavy cream
5 egg yolks   1 tablespoon vanilla
5 tablespoons granulated sugar   light brown sugar

Heat raspberries with ⅓ cup granulated sugar just until sugar is dissolved and berries have begun to yield juice. Set aside.

In electric mixer, beat egg yolks with 5 tablespoons granulated sugar until thick and lemon-colored. Beat in cornstarch.

Heat but do not boil cream in top of double boiler. Gradually add to egg yolk mixture while continuing to beat.

Return custard to double boiler and cook over simmering water, stirring constantly, until thickened (candy thermometer should reach 170°F. but no higher). Cool slightly, strain and add vanilla. Chill.

Divide raspberries among 6 4-inch custard cups. Spoon custard gently over raspberries.

Sift light brown sugar and sprinkle over top of custard, covering completely. Place custard cups under broiler only until sugar is brown and melted. Watch carefully to make sure it doesn't burn. Chill again until custard is firm and sugar has hardened.

YIELD: 6 SERVINGS

PAM WILSON'S BLUBARB PIE

pastry for a 9-inch double-crust pie made with Basic Pie Pastry (page 148)
2 cups blueberries

2 cups fresh rhubarb in 1-inch slices
1 cup sugar
3 tablespoons flour

Preheat oven to 400°F.

Roll out half the pastry as directed on page 148 and ease into a 9-inch pie pan. Trim overhang to ¾ inch. Wash, drain and sort the blueberries. Mix rhubarb and blueberries gently with the sugar and flour and spoon into pastry shell.

Roll out remaining half of dough. Ease the top crust over the filled bottom crust and trim the overhang to ¾ inch. Fold the top crust over the bottom edges and press to seal. Crimp or flute edges if desired. Make 4 triangle-shaped slits in the top crust to let steam escape. Bake for 40 to 50 minutes, or until crust is golden.

YIELD: 8 SERVINGS

ARLINE YOUNGMAN'S STRAWBERRY-HAZELNUT CAKE

This cake is not for the faint-of-heart. It contains just about everything that makes life worth living. Don't let it stand too long in the refrigerator or the sliced strawberries will "bleed."

4 egg whites
pinch of salt
1 teaspoon white vinegar
1 1/4 superfine sugar
4 teaspoons black coffee
4 1/2 ounces hazelnuts (filberts), ground

1/2 teaspoon vanilla
6 ounces (6 squares) semi-sweet chocolate
1/4 cup water
1 pint heavy cream, whipped
1 pint strawberries, sliced

Preheat oven to 300°F.

Grease and flour 2 8- or 9-inch springform pans.

Beat egg whites with salt and vinegar until they hold soft peaks. Gradually add sugar and beat until mixture is stiff and glossy. Fold in coffee, hazelnuts and vanilla. Spread meringue mixture in pans and bake about 35 minutes. Release sides of pans and cool on base of pan.

When meringues have cooled, remove from their bases and place 1 layer on a serving plate.

Melt chocolate in water and spread the layer on the serving plate with half the melted chocolate. Cover with a layer of half the whipped cream and top with sliced strawberries, reserving some for decoration.

Spread second layer of meringue with remaining chocolate and place on top of strawberry layer, chocolate side up. Cover top and sides with remaining whipped cream and refrigerate several hours. Serve decorated with reserved strawberries.

YIELD: 6 TO 8 SERVINGS

The scenario is familiar: You've picked the first ripe strawberries of the season, or you've seen them in the market, and your eyes have been bigger than your stomach. Everyone has feasted on them, and there are still a couple of pints left, looking a little shrunken and disheveled. The solution, if you don't want to go to the trouble of making jam and sealing the jars, is a strawberry purée (page 135), which is easy, freezes well, and tastes wonderful with ice cream, plain cakes and almost any sliced fruit.

FRESH RASPBERRY TRIFLE

You could substitute strawberries, blueberries or even lightly sweetened blackberries in this recipe.

soft almond macaroons or ladyfingers	*3/4 cup sugar*
2 tablespoons almond-flavored liqueur	*1 teaspoon freshly grated lemon rind*
3 cups fresh raspberries	*juice of 1/2 lemon*
5 eggs, separated	*1 tablespoon sugar*

Preheat oven to 350°F.

Line a 2-quart soufflé dish, preferably glass, with macaroons or ladyfingers. Sprinkle with liqueur.

Wash and gently dry raspberries, and spread them over the macaroons at the bottom of the dish.

Beat egg yolks with 3/4 cup sugar, lemon rind and lemon juice until thick.

Beat egg whites until stiff. Fold half of the beaten whites into the yolk mixture, and pour over the raspberries. Bake for 30 minutes or until egg mixture is firm.

Add last tablespoon of sugar to remaining whites and beat again until stiff. Spread over the top of the trifle and bake again at 325°F. for 15 minutes more or until meringue is lightly browned.

YIELD: 6 SERVINGS

BLUEBERRY-MARZIPAN TART

Use a ten-inch flan ring for your tart shell.

1 10-inch prebaked Sweet Short Tart Shell (page 147)	*1 egg, beaten*
5 tablespoons softened, unsalted butter or margarine	*1/2 teaspoon lemon rind*
1 7-ounce package almond paste, about 3/4 cup	*1 teaspoon flour*
	1 pint blueberries
	1 cup apricot preserves

Preheat oven to 350°F.

Cream butter. Add almond paste alternately with beaten egg until mixture is smooth. Stir in lemon rind and flour. Spread filling evenly in shell. Bake on lowest rack in oven for about 1 hour, or until filling is golden brown.

Pick over and wash blueberries, then pat gently dry.

In a small pan, heat apricot preserves until boiling. When tart is fully baked, spread blueberries evenly over filling and brush with apricot glaze.

YIELD: 8 SERVINGS

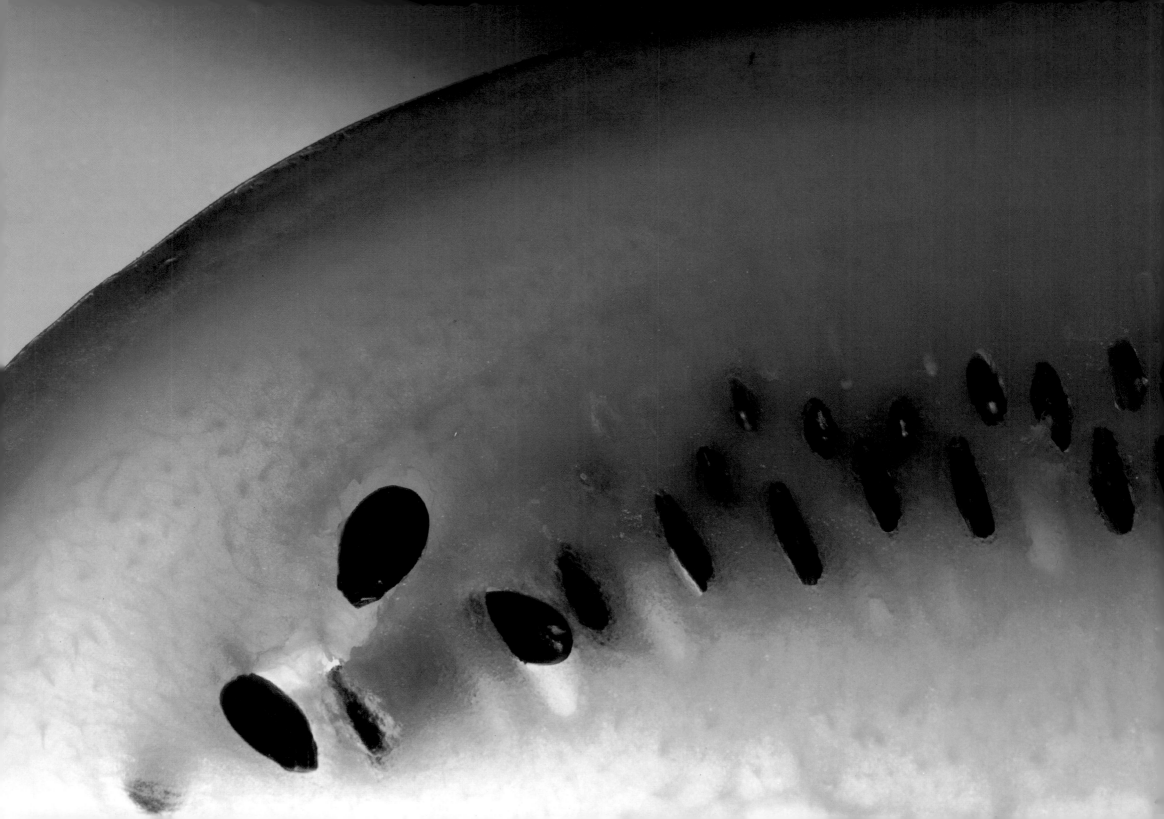

Melons and grapes are both—well, ovoid—and there's something amusing about the juxtaposition of the giants and dwarves of the fruit kingdom. Plus, they taste good together. And there the similarities end.

All melons belong to the cucumber family and grow on creeping plants that are surprisingly short—6 to 10 feet—considering the size of their offspring. Pictured in Egyptian paintings and Assyrian bas-reliefs and mentioned in the Bible, melons come from the Middle East. Until Columbus's men planted the first seeds in 1494, they were unknown in the New World.

Due to what Waverley Root calls their "exaggerated friendliness," all melons except watermelons are so quick to cross breed that

MELONS & GRAPES

growers have to plant the seeds of different species at least a quarter of a mile apart to prevent unintended hybrids. This also creates headaches for botanists, who nonetheless have described three separate groups: muskmelons, cantaloupes and winter melons.

Muskmelons, with their netting on the rind and rich aroma, are often confused with cantaloupe in the United States. True canta-loupes, grown in Europe, are not netted and are grooved like acorn squash. Winter melons, including the casabas and honeydews, ripen late in the season, store well, and unlike all other melons will get sweeter after picking. Watermelons are from a different genus of the cucumber family than the other melons and are variously claimed as native to North Africa or India.

Selecting a ripe melon may be the hardest task a fruit shopper faces. Muskmelons and cantaloupes develop a separation layer in their stems when they are pefectly ripe, allowing the melon to break off from the vine without a scar. So if there's damaged tissue where the stem has broken, chances are the melon is not ripe. There should also be some "give" at the stem end. Ripe honeydews are harder to spot—some think the seeds should rattle inside, others say to look for the yellower skins. Since honeydews ripen in storage, your odds are slightly better of getting a good one. Watermelons have the most inscrutable exteriors but, due to their giant size, they are often sold in portions. In that case you can look for good red or yellow flesh color and black seeds (unless you buy the new seedless variety, which is twice the price and only half the fun to eat).

Melons have been lavishly praised in literature, but grapes are the most celebrated by painters, appearing in art from Egyptian tomb paintings all the way through Caravaggio's *Bacchus*, nineteenth-century still-lifes, and the "fractured" Cubist grapes of Braque. There were enough native grapes growing in the New World for the Norsemen to christen it Vinland; yet when European varieties were planted on the East coast by early colonists, both climate and pests did them in. They fared much better out west, where Spanish padres established the flourishing California grape industry.

The majority of both wine and table grapes are descendants of the European *Vitis vinifera*. More than eight thousand varieties have been developed or identified. Seeded grapes generally offer more pungency and perfume, while the blander red and green Thompson seedless are unquestionably easier to use in recipes. High color and pliant stems are the best indicators of freshness, but finding a sweet grape is another matter. Greenmarket clerks won't thank me for this, but pop one in your mouth. It's the only sure way.

WATERMELON GAZPACHO

2½ pounds tomatoes, peeled and cut up (about 5 cups)	2 cups tomato juice
1 onion, cut in chunks	1 tablespoon salt
1 cup watermelon chunks, seeds removed	freshly ground pepper to taste
½ cup peeled cucumber chunks	½ cup finely chopped green pepper
1 clove garlic, chopped	½ cup finely chopped peeled cucumber
¼ cup olive oil	½ cup finely chopped watermelon, seeds removed
¼ cup white wine vinegar	optional: croutons

Mix together tomatoes, onion, watermelon, green pepper and cucumber chunks, and garlic. Purée in batches in a blender until almost smooth. Transfer to a large bowl or soup tureen and mix well with the oil and vinegar. Add tomato juice, salt and pepper. Cover and chill.

Just before serving, stir well.

Pass chopped vegetables and croutons separately so each person can add according to individual taste.

YIELD: 8 SERVINGS

CANTALOUPE WITH SMOKED CHICKEN AND RASPBERRY VINAIGRETTE

If fresh raspberries are in season, you may want to garnish this first course with a few raspberries instead of the sprouts.

½ cantaloupe	Raspberry Vinaigrette (page 145)
1 smoked chicken breast	clover sprouts or watercress

Scoop out seeds from cantaloupe half and cut into 4 equal wedges. Remove rind and cut each wedge lengthwise into 4 slices. Arrange the slices, 2 on each side facing each other like parentheses, on 4 salad plates.

Remove skin from chicken breast and slice lengthwise into ¼-inch slices. Cut each slice into julienne strips. Divide strips evenly among the 4 plates, placing them between the melon crescents.

Place a pinch of clover sprouts or a sprig of watercress at the top of the chicken strips. Drizzle melon and chicken with vinaigrette.

YIELD: 4 SERVINGS

"Chief of this world's luxuries," is the way Mark Twain described watermelon. "When one has tasted watermelon he knows what angels eat. It was not a Southern watermelon that Eve took; we know it because she repented."

CURRIED PORK LOIN
WITH HONEYDEW AND APRICOTS

The lovely apricot-colored sauce in this curry makes a nice contrast with the honeydew, but you could also use an orange melon such as cantaloupe or muskmelon. Sliced pickled ginger can be found in Oriental specialty stores.

1 1/4 pounds thick-sliced boneless pork loin	1/2 cup white wine
salt and freshly ground pepper to taste	1 tablespoon wine vinegar
1 to 2 tablespoons butter or margarine	2 tablespoons tomato paste
1/2 large onion, chopped	1/2 cup Chicken Broth (page 145)
1 large clove garlic, diced	1 bay leaf
2 teaspoons curry powder or to taste	1/2 cup dried apricots, cut in half if large
2 teaspoons brown sugar	2 teaspoons chopped pickled ginger slices
	1/4 honeydew melon

Trim fat off pork slices and cut each piece diagonally into smaller, 1/4-inch-thick slices. Season to taste with salt and pepper.

Melt butter in a large frying pan until quite hot. Sauté pork slices, turning once, until lightly browned on both sides. Remove from pan and set aside.

Add onion and garlic to pan, adding more butter if necessary, and sauté for about 5 minutes, until lightly browned. Sprinkle with curry powder and brown sugar and cook for another minute.

Pour in wine and heat over low flame, stirring to loosen all browned bits. Add vinegar, tomato paste, broth and bay leaf and stir well. Return pork to pan and add apricots and ginger. Bring sauce to a boil, reduce heat, and simmer for 5 minutes. Do not overcook or pork will get tough.

Cut the rind off the honeydew and cut flesh into bite-sized chunks. Just before serving, remove bay leaf, add honeydew chunks and heat until warm through.

YIELD: 4 SERVINGS

CANTALOUPE ICE CREAM

2 ripe cantaloupes	1 teaspoon vanilla extract
1 tablespoon fresh lemon juice	1 3/4 cups heavy cream
6 tablespoons sugar	

Cut cantaloupes in half and scoop out the seeds. Slice each half in 2, cut off the rind, and cut flesh into large chunks. Purée in a blender or food processor until smooth.

In a mixing bowl, combine purée with all other ingredients and chill.

Pour into container of ice cream maker and freeze according to manufacturer's instructions.

YIELD: ABOUT 1 1/2 QUARTS

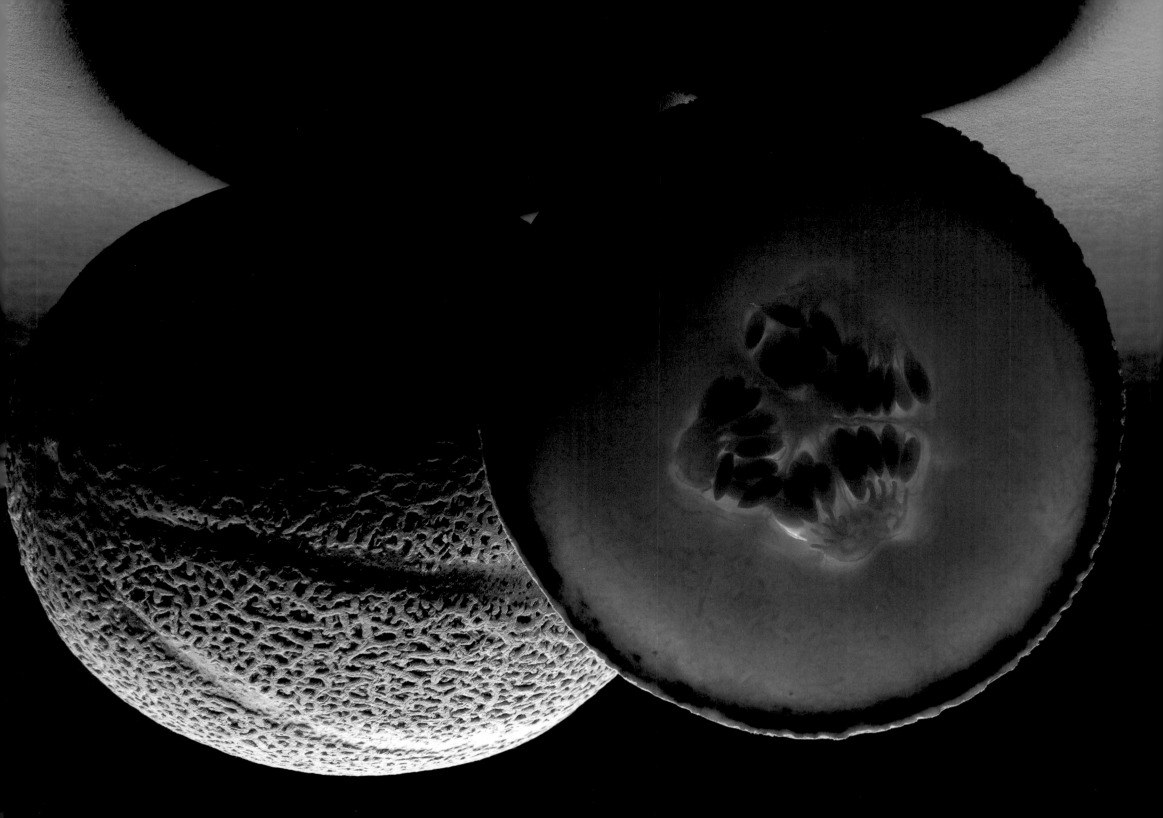

DEEP-DISH AUTUMN PIE
(WITH APPLES, PEARS AND RED GRAPES)

This pie has a festive braided trim that can be omitted if you're pressed for time, in which case you only need half the amount of pastry.

Basic Pie Pastry (page 148)
4 cups sliced, pared Cortland or
   other cooking apples
4 cups sliced, pared firm pears
3 teaspoons lemon juice
2 cups halved seedless red
   grapes
1/2 cup packed brown sugar
1/3 cup granulated sugar
2 tablespoons flour

pinch of salt
1 teaspoon grated fresh lemon
   rind
1 teaspoon cinnamon
1/2 teaspoon nutmeg
1 tablespoon butter or margarine
1 egg, lightly beaten
cinnamon sugar
optional: vanilla ice cream

Preheat over to 425°F.

Mix apples and pears and sprinkle with lemon juice. Add grapes and toss.

Blend together sugars, flour, salt, lemon rind, cinnamon and nutmeg. Toss with fruit and pour into a greased 2-quart 9- x 15-inch baking dish. Dot with bits of butter.

Roll half the pastry out to 1/4-inch thickness until it is at least 1 inch wider than pan in all directions. Place gently over fruit, overlapping dish on all sides, and trim so that pastry slightly overhangs dish. Make slits to allow steam to escape, and brush crust with beaten egg.

Roll out other half of pastry to 1/4-inch thickness and cut into long 1-inch-wide strips. Roll each strip in half lengthwise and braid three strips together at a time. Place braids around circumference of baking dish, placing them neatly, until it is completely encircled. Brush braids with egg.

Make cinnamon sugar by mixing 1 part cinnamon to 3 parts granulated sugar. Sprinkle this on pie and bake for 35 minutes, or until crust is golden brown. Serve warm, with ice cream if desired.

YIELD: 8 to 10 SERVINGS

WATERMELON SORBET

6 to 7 cups peeled and seeded
   watermelon

1/4 cup superfine sugar
juice of 1/2 lemon

Cut melon into cubes. Purée in 2 batches in blender of food processor. You should have about 4 cups of purée. Add 1/4 cup sugar and lemon juice, stir well and taste, adding more sugar if desired.

Pour into container of ice cream maker and freeze according to manufacturer's instructions.

YIELD: 1 QUART SHERBET

Most raisins come from Thompson seedless grapes; the dark ones are sun-dried, while the light ones are mechanically dehydrated and treated with sulfur dioxide to preserve their golden-amber color. California's San Joaquin Valley now produces nearly half the world's supply of raisins. Its first crop was born of an accident—a devastating heat wave in 1873 that shriveled the grapes on the vine before they could be harvested.

TWO-COLOR GRAPE TART WITH VANILLA CUSTARD FILLING

1 cup milk
1 tablespoon vanilla
1/2 pound seedless red grapes
1/2 pound seedless green grapes
1/2 cup red currant jelly

1 10-inch prebaked Sweet Short Tart Shell (page 147)
3 egg yolks
1/2 cup sugar
1/4 cup sifted flour

Beat sugar and egg yolks together for several minutes until mixture is pale yellow and very thick. Beat in flour.

In a heavy-bottomed saucepan, heat the milk to boiling and add to egg mixture in a thin stream, beating constantly with a wire whisk to incorporate. Pour mixture back into saucepan and bring to a boil, whisking continuously. The custard will get very thick. Continue cooking and whisking for a minute or 2 so the flour cooks, taking care not to scorch the custard. Remove from heat and stir in the vanilla. Transfer the custard to a bowl, place a piece of plastic wrap directly on its surface to prevent a skin from forming and cool.

When custard has cooled, spread it in the prebaked tart shell. Arrange the whole grapes, stem side down, in alternating concentric circles on top of the custard, beginning with a circle of red grapes.

Heat currant jelly to the boiling point and brush a thin coating of this glaze over the top of the tart. Refrigerate until serving time.

YIELD: 8 SERVINGS

MELON AND GRAPE MEDLEY

1 cantaloupe
1/2 honeydew melon
1 pint strawberries, stemmed
2 bananas, sliced
1 cup seedless grapes
1/2 cup chopped skinless pistachio nuts

3 pieces crystallized ginger, finely chopped
optional: superfine sugar to taste
1/2 cup freshly squeezed orange juice

Scoop out flesh of both melons with a melon-ball cutter and place in a serving bowl. Add strawberries, bananas, grapes, pistachios and ginger.

Add sugar to orange juice if desired and pour over fruit, tossing gently. Chill briefly.

YIELD: 8 SERVINGS

The Concord grape was discovered in 1845 by Ephraim W. Bull of (not surprisingly) Concord, Massachusetts, when some boys brought him seeds they had found in the woods. For a delicious fresh grape juice, squeeze ripe Concord grapes to break their skins, cover with cold water, boil until the seeds start to separate, and drain the juice through a jelly bag or cheesecloth. Dilute with two parts water and chill.

A twelve-year-old boy, who has never been to Europe, devised the name for this towering dessert. When asked how he knew about the Matterhorn he answered, "Oh, from Disneyland!"

If you keep a box of tiny amaretto cookies, Amarettini, on hand, this is a wonderful last-minute dessert for unexpected guests. It also works well with sliced peaches or bananas, and especially with fresh berries.

1 cup heavy cream, chilled
1 4.4-ounce box Amarettini di Saronno or other sweet almond-flavored biscuits

2 cups seedless red or green grapes

Whip cream until it forms soft peaks. Chill until serving time.

Crumble biscuits roughly by hand.

When ready to serve, rewhip cream briefly if necessary to restore the peaks. Mix biscuit pieces with grapes and toss gently with whipped cream. Pile high in a shallow glass dish to serve.

YIELD: 6 SERVINGS

SUSAN GIBSON'S CONCORD GRAPE PIE

The grape skins are included in this recipe because they enhance the color and texture of the pie—as they do for wine.

pastry for 9-inch deep-dish Double Crust Pie (page 148)
2 quarts blue Concord grapes (about 3 cups without the skins)

¾ cup sugar
3 to 4 tablespoons quick-cooking tapioca

Preheat oven to 400°F.

Pinch off the grape skins and save. Cook the pulp until it reaches a full rolling boil.

Strain out the seeds. Add sugar, tapioca and the skins and blend well. Pour into pie shell. Carefully place top crust on pie and seal. Cut several vents.

Bake for 45 minutes.

YIELD: 6 TO 8 SERVINGS

These are the summer fruits, since their growing season is only from May through September. South American or South African imports, picked before they are fully mature so they can withstand the rigors of shipping, simply don't pass muster no matter how desperate you are for a peach in December.

China was the original home of the peach, and the Chinese believed that if you put a bowl of peaches in a tomb, they would preserve the body from corruption until the end of time. Just before 1700, the first peach seeds arrived at the Massachusetts Bay Colony, and a century later the Spaniards brought them to California, the state that now leads the country in the production of peaches.

If J. Alfred Prufrock's "Do I dare to eat a peach?" were applied to

PEACHES, NECTARINES, PLUMS & APRICOTS

today's commercially grown peaches, the answer would often have to be a resounding "No." The best test of a ripe peach is its unmistakable fragrance. It should also yield easily to gentle hand pressure and have a yellow or creamy ground color. A reddish blush is not a sign of ripeness but the mark of certain varieties. On the other hand, a green peach will *never* ripen at home.

Food experts give short shrift to the nectarine, which they dismiss as a smooth-skinned or "fuzzless" peach. But a grower's organization insists that nectarines are a fruit unto themselves. No matter, since they are both luscious and virtually interchangeable in recipes. Ripe nectarines have the same "feel" as ripe peaches and should be richly colored.

In matters of infinite variety, the plum makes the sweet pepper look like a Johnny-come-lately. Pliny referred to *ingens turba prunorum*—the enormous crowd of plums—and indeed they are grown on every continent except Antarctica and are available in almost every imaginable hue. Over a thousand varieties are known. Some stand out for their special character: the strong-flavored damsons, the plum of Damascus; the stubborn American beach plum, which refuses to be cultivated and grows well only when left alone in poor sandy soil near the sea; and the antecedent of the greengage, the plump and highly prized green *reine-claude*. It was named after the first wife of Francis I of France, a choice Waverley Root suggests was inspired by the curves of Queen Claude's ample backside. Ripe plums should be plump and brightly colored with a slight glow or "bloom" to the skin.

The apricot is the most fragile of the stone fruits. It's hard to find a ripe one at the market, much less be lucky enough to sample one fresh from the tree, and this may account for the fruit's low popularity. The apricot has inspired some beautiful names, including "Moon of the Faithful" in eastern countries and "sun eggs" in ancient Persia. It has a peculiar facility for crossbreeding, producing the peach-apricot and the plumcot. The apricot blooms early and has a short, two-month season, during which you should look for deeply colored, relatively soft fruit without bruises. Happily, dried apricots, with a pervasive flavor, provide year-round enjoyment.

"The ripest peach is highest on the tree," wrote James Whitcomb Riley about an unattainable love. Pride of Georgia, this fruit has come to embody the complexion of the fairest of southern belles; and, in fact, Renoir advised his students to paint still lifes of peaches and apples in order to better understand the skin tones of the female breast.

PECAN WAFFLES WITH NECTARINES

Here's a recipe where peaches would work equally well.

1 cup roughly chopped pecans
2 cups sifted flour
3 teaspoons baking powder
1 teaspoon salt
2 tablespoons sugar
1 teaspoon cinnamon

2 eggs, separated
1 1/2 cups milk
6 tablespoons corn oil
4 nectarines
pure maple syrup

Preheat oven to 350°F.

Lightly toast pecans in oven; set aside to cool.

Sift together dry ingredients.

In a separate bowl, beat egg yolks. Add milk and oil, blending well. Stir into dry ingredients just long enough to moisten. Do not overbeat. Add nuts.

In a separate bowl, beat egg whites until stiff. Fold into batter.

Bake in batches in a preheated, lightly oiled waffle iron until done. Keep cooked waffles in warm oven until ready to serve. While waffles are cooking, slice nectarines and put in a serving bowl. Serve waffles with sliced nectarines and maple syrup.

YIELD: 12 4-INCH-SQUARE WAFFLES, OR 4 SERVINGS

CHILLED PEACH SOUP

6 large ripe peaches
3 tablespoons freshly squeezed lemon juice
juice of 2 oranges
1/2 cup white wine
1/2 teaspoon ground cinnamon
optional: superfine sugar
optional: 1/2 cup heavy cream for garnish
1 cup blueberries for garnish

Plunge peaches into rapidly boiling water for 10 seconds so skins peel off easily. Pit peaches and cut into chunks, then purée in small batches in a blender or food processor until smooth.

Immediately add juices to prevent discoloration. Add wine.

Put ground cinnamon in a small cup and add a bit of peach purée. Mash together so cinnamon is well blended and return to main bowl. Stir well and taste. If too tart, you can add a little superfine sugar. Chill.

If desired, whip unsweetened heavy cream until stiff and bring to table with a small bowl of blueberries. Put a dollop of cream and a handful of blueberries on each serving.

YIELD: 6 SERVINGS

APRICOT AND LAMB PILAF

A pilaf is partially-cooked rice that is combined with other cooked ingredients for the final minutes of cooking. Since the emphasis is on the rice, not the meat, it makes a light supper or a very good buffet dish.

1 large onion, chopped
1/2 cup (1 stick) butter or
  margarine
1 pound lean lamb, cut into small
  cubes
1/4 teaspoon nutmeg
1/2 teaspoon cinnamon

salt and freshly ground pepper to
  taste
1/4 cup seedless raisins
1/2 cup dried apricots
2 cups long-grain rice
1/3 cup pine nuts

Sauté onion in half the butter (4 tablespoons) until golden. Add lamb and brown on all sides. Add seasonings and fruit and stir together gently for a few minutes. Add enough water to cover, bring to a boil, and simmer gently for 1 1/2 hours, or until meat is very tender.

Cook rice separately in 4 cups boiling water until half done, about 10 minutes. Add to meat mixture with 3 additional tablespoons of the butter. Simmer gently for 20 minutes.

In a separate pan, sauté pine nuts gently in remaining tablespoon of butter and add to pilaf when rice is fully cooked.

YIELD: 8 SERVINGS

CURRIED SHRIMP WITH NECTARINES

1 medium onion, chopped
1/3 cup butter or margarine
3 tablespoons flour
1 tablespoon curry powder
1/2 teaspoon salt
1/8 teaspoon white pepper

1 1/2 cups milk
3 to 4 fresh nectarines
1 pound medium shrimp, shelled
  and deveined
3 tablespoons dry sherry
1 cup fresh or frozen peas, cooked

Sauté onion in butter until transparent. Stir in flour, curry powder, salt and pepper. Add milk gradually. Cook, stirring, over medium heat until mixture thickens and comes to a boil. Remove from heat and reserve.

Slice nectarines to measure 2 cups.

Cook shrimp in 1 cup water only until they turn pink. Drain well.

Fold nectarines, shrimp, sherry and peas into sauce. Heat thoroughly and serve over rice.

YIELD: 4 SERVINGS

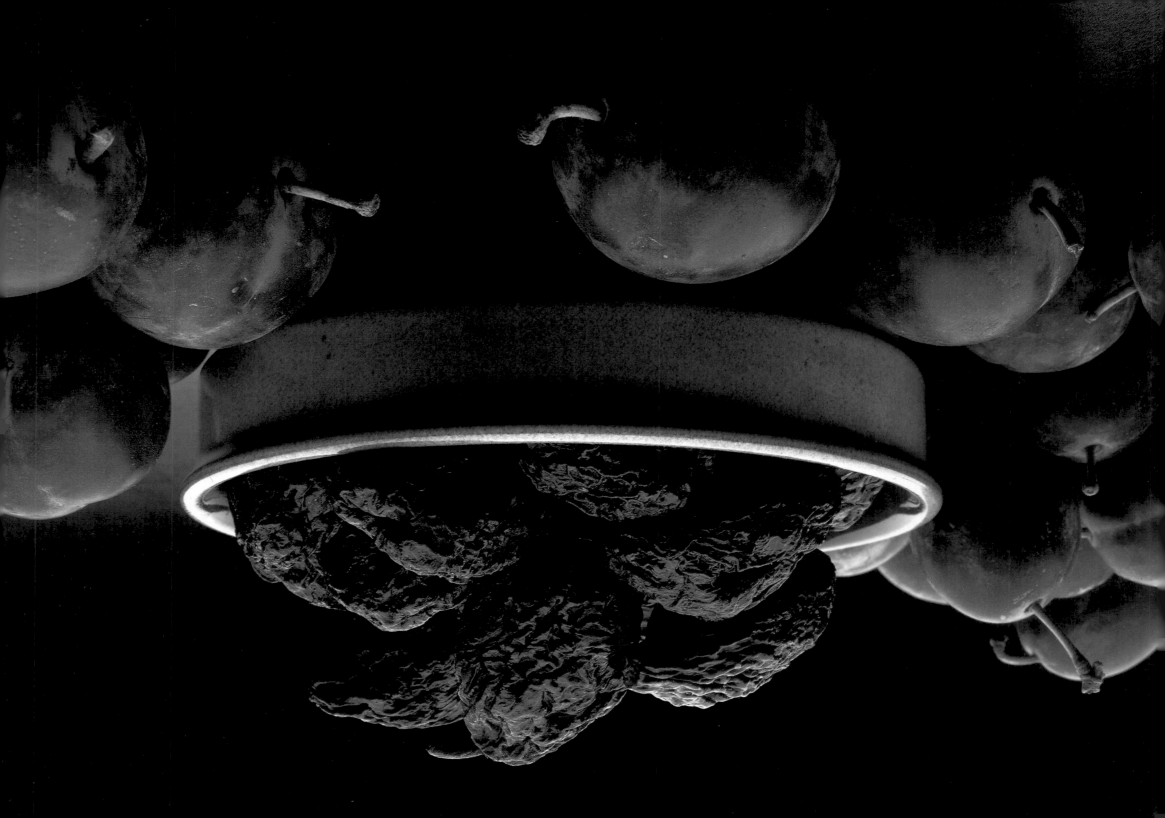

Anyone who has sampled a ripe summer plum knows why the word is also used to mean a choice object or an unexpected windfall. The contrast between the plum's tart skin and sweet flesh sets it apart from other summer fruit. And its inside is always a mystery: a yellow plum may be red-fleshed, a red may be yellow, a blue may be green. Only its consumer knows for sure.

PLUM-LEMON PUFF PUDDING

In this miracle dessert, a lemon custard forms at the bottom of the dish, a baked "soufflé" at the top!

3/4 pound fresh plums, quartered
    and pitted
1/4 cup water
1/4 cup sugar
pinch of cinnamon
1 teaspoon cornstarch dissolved
    in 1 tablespoon brandy
4 tablespoons (1/2 stick) butter or
    margarine

1/2 cup sugar
grated rind of 1 lemon
2 eggs, separated
3 tablespoons fresh lemon juice
3 tablespoons flour
1 cup milk

Combine plums, water, sugar and cinnamon in a saucepan and bring to a boil over moderate heat. Reduce heat and simmer for 5 minutes. Blend in cornstarch-brandy mixture. Continue cooking for 2 minutes more, stirring constantly. Pour this mixture into a 1-quart baking dish. Let cool for about 30 minutes.

Preheat oven to 375°F.

Cream butter, sugar and lemon rind. Add egg yolks, beating well. Add lemon juice, mixing well, and then the flour and milk. Beat until smooth. In a separate bowl, beat egg whites until stiff. Fold into yolk mixture and pour over the prepared fruit.

Place baking dish inside a larger pan containing 1 inch of boiling water. Bake for 45 minutes, until the top is golden brown and set. Serve hot or cold.

YIELD: 4 SERVINGS

EDITH'S OLD-FASHIONED PEACH CAKE

I've never seen a recipe that called for $1^{7}/_{8}$ cups of anything, but the experienced baker who bequeathed me this recipe insisted on the measurement. And it works. If you want to "gild the peach," you can glaze this cake with apricot jam pressed through a sieve and heated briefly with a little water and lemon extract. You can also use plums or nectarines in this cake.

$1^{7}/_{8}$ cups flour
$1^{1}/_{2}$ teaspoons baking powder
4 tablespoons sugar
1/2 cup (1 stick) butter or
    margarine
1 egg

1 teaspoon lemon juice
1 teaspoon vanilla extract
2 pounds ripe peaches
3 to 4 tablespoons sugar
1/4 teaspoon cinnamon
1/4 teaspoon almond extract

Sift together flour, baking powder and sugar. With a pastry blender or 2 knives, cut in butter until mixture resembles coarse meal. Beat the egg with the lemon juice and vanilla until frothy and pour into the flour mixture, adding a little water if necessary to make a soft dough. Knead briefly and refrigerate in wax paper for 1 hour.

Preheat oven to 350°F.

Press the dough into a greased 9-inch springform pan. Build up the sides about $1^{1}/_{4}$ inches so a valley is formed in the middle. Slice peaches and arrange in a petal formation, in two layers if necessary. Sprinkle with sugar, cinnamon and almond extract.

Bake for about 30 minutes, or until pastry is golden and peaches are tender. Cool on a rack, then release from springform.

YIELD: 8 SERVINGS

APRICOT MARZIPAN TORTE

A torte is a rich cake, especially one that has little or no flour, as opposed to a tart, which has a pastry shell.

1/2 cup (1 stick) butter or margarine
7 ounces marzipan (sweetened almond paste)
3 eggs
1/2 teaspoon almond extract

10 fresh apricots
3 tablespoons apricot jam
optional: 1 tablespoon almond-flavored liqueur
1/2 cup cake flour, sifted

Preheat oven to 350°F.

Cream together butter and marzipan, making sure that no lumps remain. Add eggs, one at a time, beating well after each addition. Stir in almond extract. Pour into a buttered and floured 9-inch springform pan, spreading evenly.

Halve apricots along their length and pit them. Arrange them skin side up on the surface of the cake. Bake for 45 minutes, or until a toothpick inserted in the center comes out clean.

When cake comes out of oven, heat apricot jam and liqueur over medium heat until syrupy; strain and brush over top of cake. Release cake from springform when cool.

YIELD: 8 SERVINGS

ANDREA'S PLUM COBBLER

3/4 pound fresh plums, halved and pitted
2 tablespoons brown sugar
2 tablespoons granulated sugar
1 teaspoon grated orange peel
pinch of cinnamon

1 teaspoon cornstarch dissolved in 2 teaspoons brandy
1/2 cup heavy cream
2 eggs, separated
3 tablespoons granulated sugar
pinch of cinnamon
1/2 cup finely chopped walnuts

Preheat oven to 350°F.

Combine plums, brown sugar, 2 tablespoons granulated sugar, orange peel and cinnamon in a saucepan. Add 1/4 cup water and bring to a boil over moderate heat. Reduce heat to low and simmer 5 minutes. Blend in cornstarch mixture and continue cooking for 2 minutes more, stirring constantly.

Pour mixture into a greased 1-quart baking dish.

Beat together heavy cream, egg yolks, egg sugar, 3 tablespoons granulated sugar and another pinch of cinnamon until smooth.

In a separate bowl, beat egg whites until they form soft peaks and fold into cream mixture along with chopped walnuts. Spoon carefully over fruit. Bake for 30 minutes, or until topping is golden brown.

YIELD: 6 SERVINGS

Since apricots travel badly and do not keep, they are rare when fresh—but worth waiting for, not only for their taste. Their vitamin A content is a hundred times greater than the average in other fruits. As a result, the fruit helps us combat night blindness. It is also beneficial to dry skin, in the form of apricot pulp mashed with a little oil to make a facial masque.

JOHN'S BIRTHDAY CAKE
(PRUNE CAKE WITH CARAMEL FROSTING)

If prunes sound awful to you, don't worry: They virtually disappear into this moist spice cake, which is a snap to make in the food processor. The frosting is a little tricky. Don't make it until after the cake has cooled since it hardens fast and must be spread immediately.

1 cup stewed prunes, halved and pitted	1 teaspoon baking powder
4 eggs	1 teaspoon baking soda
1½ cups granulated sugar	
1 cup (2 sticks) butter or margarine	**Frosting**
1 cup buttermilk	1½ cups brown sugar, packed
2 cups flour	1½ cups granulated sugar
½ teaspoon cinnamon	1½ cups milk
½ teaspoon allspice	2 tablespoons butter or margarine

Preheat oven to 375°F.

Place prunes, eggs, granulated sugar, butter and buttermilk in a food processor and process until smooth.

Sift together dry ingredients and add to processor in small batches through feed tube, processing only until flour disappears.

Divide batter between 2 buttered and floured 9-inch cake pans and bake for 30 minutes, or until toothpick inserted in middle comes out clean. (Do not overbake—cake should be moist.) Invert layers on racks to cool.

After the cake is thoroughly cool, make the frosting: In a heavy-bottomed 2½-quart pan (mixture will foam up to fill this space), combine sugars and milk and bring to a boil, stirring constantly. Cook over high heat *without stirring* until syrup reaches 232°F. on a candy thermometer and a small amount forms a very soft ball in cold water.

Add butter, remove from heat and cool to lukewarm (110°F.). Beat until thick and creamy, to right consistency for spreading. If necessary, you can place bowl over hot water to keep frosting soft enough while spreading.

YIELD: 12 OR MORE SERVINGS

PEACH SORBET

The flavor of this sorbet is so intense that it's the second best thing to biting into a ripe peach itself—and perhaps better, on a blistering hot day.

7 to 8 ripe, local, medium-sized peaches, unpeeled (about 2 pounds)	1 tablespoon lemon juice
	½ cup sugar
	2 tablespoons light corn oil

Quarter peaches, discard pits and purée the fruit in a blender or food processor. You should have about 3½ cups of purée.

Combine purée, lemon juice, sugar and corn oil in a bowl and chill thoroughly.

Pour into container of an ice cream maker and freeze according to manufacturer's instructions.

YIELD: ABOUT 1 QUART

Never underestimate the power of the apple, which allegedly caused Adam and Eve to be expelled from the Garden of Eden, created the rivalry that brought about the Trojan War, helped Sir Isaac Newton discover the law of gravity, and inspired countless fighting men in World War II as the principal ingredient in Mom's pie. Through the ages, the apple has been a kind of universal standard of reference for suspicious-looking new fruits and vegetables. When they first appeared in Europe, both lemons and peaches were called Persian apples, eggplants were "mad apples," tomatoes, "love apples," and the French named potatoes *pommes de terre,* or earth apples.

Back to the Garden of Eden, for a moment. Generations of artists

APPLES, PEARS & A PERSIMMON OR TWO

have represented the apple as the forbidden fruit, but Genesis refers only to the "fruit of the tree of knowledge." According to biblical scholars, the ancient Hebrews would more likely have chosen the pomegranate had someone asked them to be specific about the tempting fruit. Turn-of-the-century humorist Ambrose Bierce,

unaware of this bit of scholarship, thought Adam was justly thrown out of Paradise: the first apple, says Bierce, was a crab apple and "the first man was an idiot for eating it."

Governor Endicott of the Massachusetts Bay Colony was the first apple grower in the United States. Johnny Appleseed, who really existed in the person of John Chapman, a self-styled missionary, established apple nurseries from the Alleghenies all the way west to the Mississippi. Out of his early work, there are now over a hundred varieties of apples grown commercially in this country.

From Gravenstein to Golden Delicious, from Northern Spy to Rome Beauty and Macoun to Mutsu, there's a favorite for every taste. Even runty little crab apples can be used to make jelly. Lacking your own tree, you'll find the best apples at orchards and farm stands. The color depends upon the variety you choose, but you can't go wrong with apples that are firm and free of bruises.

The pear could be called the grandfather of the apple, inasmuch as it was cultivated earlier and comes from the same family—*Rosaceae*—though not from the same genus. Pliny catalogued forty-one varieties of pear, and the numbers have proliferated since then. The smooth juicy Bartletts are the summer pears and most common in this country. Winter brings the Boscs with their speckled, rusty color and tapered neck; the buttery, fragrant Comice, considered too "fine" to use for cooking; and the Anjou with their chubby necks and spicy, rich flavor.

The latter hail from a long line of distinguished French pears. Perhaps their golden age was the reign of Louis XIV and his superintendent of orchards, La Quintinie, a lawyer-turned-gardener whose passion for raising pears matched the king's own for eating them. Royal favorites had such tantalizing names as *cuisse-madame* ("my lady's thigh") and *brute bonne* (very roughly, "ugly, but delicious").

The persimmon found in American markets is usually the Japanese variety (which originated in China), a large, plump, heart-shaped fruit. The native American persimmon is only the size of a cherry tomato.

When ripe, the persimmon contains more natural sugar than any other tree fruit and should be very soft, glossy and deeply colored. Never try biting into a hard persimmon, or your mouth may be permanently puckered. Elizabeth Schneider, in her very useful book Uncommon Fruits and Vegetables, advises looking for persimmons that are ''softer than baby cheeks (almost liquid)." They can be ripened at home just like pears. Adding a banana or apple to the bag will hasten the process.

Today's surviving strains sound woefully dull by comparison.

Commercially grown pears are not allowed to ripen on the tree not only because they are fragile but because the tree-ripened fruit tends to get woody or gritty. You can ripen them at home by placing the pears in a loosely closed paper bag and storing them at room temperature. This allows the fruits' naturally produced ethylene gas to do the trick. Check them daily—the peak can come and go in a few hours—and refrigerate when ripe.

The persimmon has no business whatsoever in this section, except that its growing season—late autumn—roughly coincides with the apple and the pear. Also called kaki, it is the ultimate late-bloomer among fruits, ripening around the first frost when its deep orange hue provides a welcome flash of color on the leafless trees.

PEAR VELVET SOUP

This soup has a lovely, subtle flavor but it is quite rich. Serve in shallow bowls so you won't overwhelm your audience.

4 medium potatoes, peeled
4 pears, peeled and cored
3 tablespoons butter or margarine
4 cups Chicken Broth (page 145)
1 cinnamon stick

$^{1}/_{2}$ teaspoon salt
optional: pinch of sugar
$^{1}/_{2}$ cup heavy cream
white pepper to taste
currant or raspberry preserves

Cut potatoes and pears into cubes of equal size. Melt butter in a large skillet and sauté potatoes and pears, stirring occasionally, for about 5 minutes.

Transfer to a 4-quart pot and add chicken broth, cinnamon stick, salt and—if pears were not very ripe—a pinch of sugar. Bring to a boil, cover and simmer about 10 minutes, or until cubes are tender.

Purée in batches in a blender or food processor until very smooth, and return to pot. Add cream and white pepper. Heat gently, without boiling, before serving and swirl a dollop of preserves into each bowl as you bring it to the table.

YIELD: 8 SERVINGS

APPLE-SMOTHERED PORK CHOPS

6 lean loin pork chops, about
   1 inch thick
$^{1}/_{2}$ teaspoon salt
$^{1}/_{2}$ teaspoon sage
3 tart apples
2 tablespoons molasses

3 tablespoons flour
$1^{1}/_{2}$ cups hot water
1 tablespoon vinegar
$^{1}/_{2}$ teaspoon salt
fresh ground pepper to taste
$^{1}/_{3}$ cup raisins

Preheat oven to 350°F.

Sprinkle pork chops with salt and sage and brown slowly on both sides in their own fat in a heavy skillet. Place in a baking dish that just accommodates them.

Pare, core and slice apples in $^{1}/_{4}$-inch slices or rings and arrange on top of chops. Drizzle molasses over the apples.

Add flour to the fat in skillet, and cook until brown, stirring constantly. Add the water and stir until mixture comes to a boil and thickens. Add vinegar, salt, pepper and raisins. Pour over apples and chops. Cover and bake until apples are tender, about 40 minutes.

YIELD: 6 SERVINGS

CURRIED CHICKEN AND GREEN APPLE SALAD

This recipe serves a crowd, but it can easily be adapted for a smaller amount of chicken.

1 large roasting chicken, 6 to 7 pounds
4 cups Mayonnaise (pages 145–46)
2 teaspoons lemon juice
4 teaspoons curry powder (or to taste)
salt and freshly ground pepper to taste

4 cups chopped celery
1 onion, peeled and halved
2 carrots, scraped and trimmed
4 celery stalks with leaves
2 sprigs parsley
salt and freshly ground pepper to taste

6 cups chopped green apples (about 3 large)

Place chicken, onion, carrots and celery in a large stockpot and cover with cold water. Add parsley and salt and pepper. Bring to a boil and simmer, partially covered, until chicken is tender, about 1½ to 2 hours.

Cool chicken in the broth. Strain broth and reserve for another use.

Remove the chicken meat from the bones and cut into bite-sized pieces. You should have about 8 cups. Combine chicken with apples and chopped celery. Mix mayonnaise with lemon juice, curry powder, salt and pepper and toss lightly with chicken mixture. Chill.

YIELD: 12 OR MORE SERVINGS

Red Delicious: Even the name is a marketing ploy! Discovered in 1872 by Jesse Hiatt of Peru, Iowa, who called it the "Hawkeye," this apple was renamed by the commercial nursery that bought the propagation rights in 1894. By far the most widely planted variety of apple in the United States today, the Red Delicious, set apart by its broad shoulders and knobby base, is largely an eating apple. Try chopping it up into apple muffins to take advantage of its bright red skin and juicy texture.

APPLE, CHEESE AND CIDER MUFFINS

Use Red Delicious apples for this recipe. Core but don't peel them before grating.

1½ cups flour
½ cup sugar
½ teaspoon salt
1 cup coarsely grated apples
¾ cup quick-cooking oats
1 teaspoon baking powder
1 teaspoon baking soda

2 eggs
¾ cup apple cider
½ teaspoon ground ginger
½ cup (1 stick) butter or margarine
¾ cup coarsely grated sharp Cheddar cheese

Preheat oven to 400°F.

Cream butter and sugar until fluffy. Add eggs 1 at a time, beating well after each addition.

In another bowl, mix and sift dry ingredients. Add alternately with cider to butter mixture, beating only until blended. Stir in apples, oats and cheese.

Fill well greased muffin tins ⅔ full. Bake for 25 minutes.

YIELD: 15 MUFFINS

You can count on green apples to be tart, crisp and juicy, even if you can't get apple lovers to agree on which variety is best. There are the Rhode Island Greening, the Newton Pippin and the Granny Smith, which turned up in Australia in 1867 when Marie Ann Smith (can you guess her nickname?) discovered a new seedling at the edge of her orchard in a Sydney suburb.

STEFANIE AKSELROD'S APPLE TORTE

1 cup flour
1 cup granulated sugar
3 tablespoons brown sugar
$1/2$ cup (1 stick) butter or
   margarine
2 teaspoons vanilla

1 8-ounce package cream
   cheese, softened
1 egg
2 large apples
1 teaspoon cinnamon
pinch of nutmeg
$1/2$ cup sliced blanched almonds

Mix flour, $1/3$ cup of the granulated sugar and the brown sugar. Add butter in pieces and 1 teaspoon of the vanilla. Work with fingers or pastry blender until mixture resembles coarse meal. Chill briefly, then press into a 9-inch springform pan, building up the edges about 1 inch all around.

Preheat oven to 450°F.

With electric beater, mix cream cheese, egg, $1/3$ cup of the granulated sugar, and remaining vanilla until smooth. Spread over crust. Peel apples and slice thickly. Toss with remaining sugar, cinnamon and nutmeg. Arrange apples over cream cheese layer and sprinkle almonds evenly on top.

Bake 10 minutes at 450°F., reduce heat to 425°F. and bake another 20 minutes. Reduce heat again to 400°F. and bake 15 to 20 minutes more, or until a knife inserted in the center comes out clean. Cool cake and chill at least 4 hours before serving.

YIELD: 8 SERVINGS

JENNI KENT'S APPLE CAKE WITH BROWN SUGAR GLAZE

This cake, though simple to make, is rich and delicious. You can, if you want to cut calories, eliminate the topping.

3 cups flour
1 teaspoon baking soda
1 teaspoon cinnamon
$1/4$ teaspoon salt
3 eggs
$1^1/2$ cups vegetable oil
2 cups granulated sugar

2 teaspoons vanilla
3 cups thickly sliced pared apples
1 cup chopped walnuts
1 cup brown sugar
$1/4$ cup milk
$1/2$ cup (1 stick) butter or
   margarine

Preheat oven to 350°F.

Sift together flour, soda, cinnamon and salt.

In a large bowl beat eggs, oil and granulated sugar at high speed for 3 minutes. Slowly add dry ingredients, then stir in vanilla. Batter will be very stiff. Fold in apples and nuts.

Turn into a greased and floured 10-inch tube pan and bake for $1^1/4$ hours.

Just before removing cake from oven, boil together the brown sugar, milk and butter for 3 minutes. When cake is removed, pour hot topping over hot cake. Let cool in pan.

YIELD: 12 OR MORE SERVINGS

PEAR GINGERBREAD

1 tablespoon lemon juice
1 scant cup milk
1½ cups sifted flour
½ cup sugar
½ teaspoon baking powder
½ teaspoon baking soda
½ teaspoon salt
1½ teaspoons ground ginger
1 teaspoon cinnamon
¼ teaspoon nutmeg
¼ teaspoon allspice

1 egg
4 tablespoons (½ stick) melted
   butter or margarine
¼ cup maple syrup
2 large ripe pears
1 teaspoon sugar
¼ teaspoon cinnamon
2 tablespoons butter or margarine
1 cup heavy cream
1 tablespoon superfine sugar

Place lemon juice into a measuring cup and fill to the 1-cup measure with milk. Stir well and let stand for at least 10 minutes to make sour milk

Sift together the dry ingredients and spices.

In a separate smaller bowl, beat the egg and add melted butter, maple syrup and sour milk; mix well.

Preheat oven to 350°F.

Add the liquid ingredients to the dry ones and beat for 2 minutes, or until batter is creamy. Spoon into a greased and floured 9-inch-square baking pan.

Peel pears and chop fine—you should have about 2 heaping cups. Spread pears gently and evenly on top of batter. Combine sugar and cinnamon and sprinkle over pears. Dot with butter.

Bake for 40 to 45 minutes, or until center of cake springs back when touched lightly. (Do not overbake—cake should be moist.)

Just before serving, whip heavy cream, add superfine sugar and blend well. Put a dollop of cream on each serving.

YIELD: 9 SERVINGS

Here's a recipe that is sufficiently delicate to bring out the subtle, elusive flavor of the persimmon. It's also low in cholesterol. Use very ripe persimmons or you won't get the full flavor.

4 to 6 very ripe persimmons	1 tablespoon freshly squeezed
pinch of salt	lemon juice
1/3 cup sugar, preferably superfine	1/4 teaspoon cinnamon
3 egg whites	optional: crumbled Gingersnaps-from-Scratch (page 93) for garnish

Cut persimmons in half. Scoop out pulp with a spoon and purée in electric blender or food processor. You should have 1 1/2 cups.

Add salt, cinnamon and lemon juice to purée and blend well.

Beat egg whites with sugar until stiff. Fold in persimmon mixture. Chill until serving time. Serve in glass bowls or sundae dishes with crumbled ginger-snaps on top.

YIELD: 6 TO 8 SERVINGS

These pears make a beautiful display and, needless to say, the mixture of flavors is sensational. They will keep in the refrigerator for up to thirty-six hours without "weeping."

8 slightly underripe pears with stems intact	piece of lemon peel
6 ounces semi-sweet chocolate	4 tablespoons (1/2 stick) sweet butter or margarine
2 cinnamon sticks	fresh or crystallized mint, or firm green leaves for garnish
3 cups of red wine	
8 whole cloves	
1 cup sugar	

Peel pears, leaving stems intact, and drop each one as peeled into cold water containing a little lemon juice to prevent discoloring.

In a large enamel saucepan, heat wine, cinnamon sticks, cloves, sugar and lemon peel until sugar dissolves. Add pears and simmer, partially covered, until tender when pierced with a knife, about 30 to 40 minutes. Cool in syrup and chill overnight.

Melt chocolate and butter in a double boiler and stir until mixture is smooth.

Remove pears from syrup and dry gently with a paper towel. Trim bottoms if necessary to help them stand upright.

Dip pears in chocolate mixture and coat evenly (use a spoon if necessary). Lift pears to drain excess chocolate and place standing on serving dish. Garnish with mint or leaves.

YIELD: 8 SERVINGS

The Boscs are the Borzois of the pear family—long, slender and tapered, by far the most elegantly shaped. But if American pear growers have their way, the pears of the future may be red: The success of the red Bartlett, which is more resistant to disease and commands a higher price than other types, has led growers to cultivate red Comice and Anjou varieties.

SOUTH CAROLINA PERSIMMON PUDDING

This is an adaptation of a traditional dense, old-fashioned dessert. Unfortunately, it obscures the delicate flavor of the persimmons but is quite tasty nonetheless. It resembles Indian pudding and can be mixed by hand, without an electric mixer. Use persimmons that are really soft, a moment before they spoil.

3 very ripe persimmons
4 tablespoons (1/2 stick) butter or
   margarine
3/4 cup firmly packed brown sugar
1 cup milk
1 cup flour

2 teaspoons baking powder
1/4 teaspoon salt
1/2 teaspoon cinnamon
1/4 teaspoon nutmeg
1 cup heavy cream, whipped with
   1 tablespoon granulated sugar

Preheat oven to 325°F.

Cut persimmons in half. Scoop out the pulp with a spoon and purée in an electric blender or food processor. You should have about 1 cup of purée.

Melt butter and stir in sugar until dissolved. Combine with persimmon purée and milk.

Sift together flour, baking powder, salt, cinnamon and nutmeg and stir into persimmon mixture until smooth.

Pour into a buttered 1-quart baking dish and bake for about 1 hour, or until pudding begins to pull away from edge of dish but is still soft on surface. Serve warm with whipped cream.

YIELD: 6 SERVINGS

Now somewhat exotic, persimmons were commonplace to early Americans, who used them for beer, bread, pudding and salads. This native American fruit and its Japanese counterpart are luscious and sweet when soft and ripe, but when green "will drawe a mans mouth awrie with much torment," as John Smith discovered when he bit into one too soon.

These are the exotics, the fruits that lend a bit of glamour to a fruit salad and give off an air of faraway lands.

Like the apple, the banana figures in the Garden of Eden controversy. A Hindu legend identifies it as the forbidden fruit and says that the first man and woman covered their nakedness with banana leaves (which, one has to admit, would do a more comprehensive job than apple or fig leaves). The banana probably originated in southern Asia; Arab traders whisked it off to Africa, where the word "banana" was coined; and in 1516 a Spanish missionary, Tomás de Berlanga, carried the first banana roots to the Americas.

Bananas grow on the world's tallest plant without a woody trunk—it's an herb, in fact, not a tree. They develop their best eating quality

BANANAS, PINEAPPLES, COCONUTS, PAPAYAS & KIWIS

after harvesting and will ripen at room temperature. Shop for plump fruit that is not bruised or split, whose yellow skin is lightly speckled with brown.

Unlike so many other new foods that were greeted with suspicion by Europeans, the pineapple won immediate acceptance when Columbus presented it to Queen Isabella in 1493. It quickly became a sign of wealth and luxury and a symbol of hospitality. Columbus called it *piña de Indes* because it resembled a giant pine cone. This inspired its English name and another tribute to the ubiquitous apple.

If you've ever tasted a pineapple in Hawaii, Mexico or the Caribbean, an import will never satisfy you again. No matter what the grocer may tell you, pineapples cannot sweeten after picking. And the fully ripe fruits are too fragile to be shipped. The best you can do is to buy pineapples that have been rushed in by air. Look for a bright yellow-gold shell color and the characteristic fragrance. Plucking a leaf from the crown will tell you nothing about the quality of the flesh.

Marco Polo called the coconut "Pharaoh's nut," alluding to its Egyptian past. In Sanskrit the palm on which it grows is called "tree which gives all that is necessary for living." Not only is its wood and fruit useful, but also its leaves—for roofing; its oil—for soaps, perfumes and cosmetics; and even its young buds are savored as a delicacy. A ripe coconut is full of juice (not to be confused with coconut milk, the liquid derived from grated coconut meat)—you should hear it slosh when you shake it.

The papaya's alternate name, tree-melon, is wrong on two counts: It is no melon, and the stalk on which it grows is an herbaceous plant. Papaya contains a remarkable enzyme, papain, that makes tough meat tender and is used in commercial tenderizers. Skeptical? The next time you cook a tough pot roast, add a little papaya juice. Papayas will ripen somewhat at home, but look for a good yellow color and some "give" to the touch.

The kiwi, with its shock of inner green, is said to be a native of China. It has flourished in New Zealand for many years and is now grown commercially in California. It was originally called Chinese gooseberry, but in the McCarthy-mad atmosphere of the 1950s, when it was first introduced, Americans would have nothing to do with a Communist fruit. So New Zealanders renamed it for their national bird. Kiwis contain the same tenderizing enzyme as papaya. Buy kiwis firm; they will ripen at room temperature.

RHODA'S GRANOLA

Caution: This homemade cereal has a lot of healthy ingredients, but it's also full of calories. You can use half dark, half golden raisins to make it more colorful.

4 cups quick-cooking rolled oats	2 tablespoons brown sugar
2 cups wheat germ	1 teaspoon salt
1 cup shredded dried coconut	½ cup honey
1 cup sliced almonds	3 tablespoons sesame seeds
1½ teaspoons cinnamon	1 teaspoon vanilla
	½ cup corn oil
	1½ cups raisins

Preheat oven to 350°F.

Mix first 8 dry ingredients. Add honey and mix well. Add vanilla to oil, mix and combine thoroughly with other ingredients.

Spread on an ungreased 10- x 15-inch jelly-roll pan and bake for 30 minutes, stirring occasionally. Remove from oven and stir in raisins. When cool, store in a covered container.

YIELD: ABOUT 12 CUPS

BANANA PANCAKES WITH PAPAYA SLICES AND LIME

This may sound like a lot of sugar, but in fact the pancakes are not overly sweet. If the papaya and lime topping doesn't interest you, the pancakes alone are delicious with the traditional butter and maple syrup.

1 ripe papaya	1 tablespoon corn oil
½ teaspoon salt	1 very ripe medium-sized banana
2 teaspoons baking soda	2 eggs
1 cup buttermilk	1 lime, quartered
1 cup sifted flour	confectioners' sugar
	1 tablespoon granulated sugar

Cut papaya in half lengthwise, pare skin and scoop out seeds. Cut both halves into crosswise slices and set aside. The fruit will not discolor when exposed to air.

Add baking soda to buttermilk and stir to dissolve.

In a medium-sized bowl, mash banana well with a fork. Crack eggs into the bowl and beat until combined. Add sugar, salt, oil and buttermilk mixture and stir well. Add flour and stir only until flour is moistened. Batter will be a bit lumpy.

Preheat griddle or large frying pan and brush lightly with oil. Drop batter by serving-spoonfuls onto griddle. Turn when edges begin to look dry and top develops air bubbles. Cook 2 or 3 minutes on second side—these pancakes will take longer to cook through than the ordinary kind.

Top each serving with papaya slices. Sprinkle them with lime juice and confectioners' sugar that has been pressed through a strainer.

YIELD: 4 SERVINGS (16 3-INCH PANCAKES)

Bananas are now the world's most widely consumed fruit. A 1971 survey showed that Americans managed to polish off 18 1/2 pounds per person per year, and one can only guess at what we've consumed since. Contrary to what Chiquita, the animated banana of the 1940s, told housewives in her advertising jingles, bananas can be refrigerated for a few days after ripening. The skin will turn brown, but no harm will come to the fruit inside.

ABOUT THE AUTHOR

CAROL E. SCHNEIDER is a graduate of Wellesley College. She is the author of fourteen editions of the popular and much-praised *The Food Calendar.* She lives in Scarsdale, New York, with her three sons.

SOURCES

Bartlett, John. *Bartlett's Familiar Quotations,* 14th Ed. Boston: Little, Brown and Company 1968.

Bianchini, Francesco, Francesco Corbetta and Marilena Pistoia. *The Complete Book of Fruits and Vegetables.* New York: Crown Publishers, 1975.

Bierce, Ambrose. *The Enlarged Devil's Dictionary,* compiled and ed. Ernest J. Hopkins. New York: Doubleday & Co., 1967.

Brown, Dale. *American Cooking,* Foods of the World Series. New York: Time-Life, 1968.

Claiborne, Craig. *The New York Times Food Encyclopedia.* New York: Times Books, 1985.

Claiborne, Craig with Pierre Franey. "Garlic's Magical Bite." *The New York Times Magazine,* February 17, 1985.

The Editors of American Heritage. *The American Heritage Cookbook.* New York: American Heritage Publishing Company, 1964.

Fussell, Betty. "Pumpkin Time." *The New York Times Magazine,* October 30, 1983.

Green, Jonathon, ed. *Consuming Passions.* New York: Fawcett Columbine, 1985.

Grigson, Jane. *Jane Grigson's Fruit Book.* New York: Atheneum, 1982.

Grigson, Jane. *Jane Grigson's Vegetable Book.* New York: Atheneum, 1979.

Jones, Evan. *American Food: The Gastronomic Story.* New York: E. P. Dutton, 1975.

Lang, Jennifer Harvey, ed. *Larousse Gastronomique.* New York: Crown Publishers, 1988.

Langseth-Christensen, Lillian. "Horseradish." *Gourmet,* April 1978.

"Lentils." Gastronomie Sans Argent, *Gourmet,* March 1981.

Lovelock, Yann. *The Vegetable Book.* New York: St. Martin's Press, 1973.

Morash, Marian. *The Victory Garden Cookbook.* New York: Alfred A. Knopf, 1982.

Parrish, Marlene. "The Piquant Pleasures of Ginger." *The Pleasures of Cooking,* undated.

Radecka, Helena. *The Fruit and Nut Book.* New York: McGraw-Hill Book Company, 1984.

Rian, Sarah Belk. "Peas." *The Cook's Magazine,* May/June 1984.

Root, Waverley. *Food.* New York: Simon & Schuster, A Fireside Book, 1980.

Schneider, Elizabeth. *Uncommon Fruits and Vegetables.* New York: Harper & Row, 1986.

Seilig, R. A. *Selection and Care of Fresh Fruits and Vegetables.* Washington: United Fresh Fruit and Vegetable Association, undated.

Seranne, Ann and John Tebbel. *The Epicure's Companion.* New York: David McKay Company, 1962.

Stobart, Tom. *The Cook's Encyclopedia.* New York: Harper & Row, 1981.

Strouse, Jean. "The World According to Garlic." *The New York Times Magazine,* December 9, 1979.

Tannahill, Reay. *Food in History.* New York: Stein & Day, 1973.

Trager, James. *The Enriched, Fortified, Concentrated, Country-Fresh, Lip-Smacking, Finger-Licking, International, Unexpurgated Foodbook.* New York: Grossman Publishers, 1978.

Trillin, Calvin. *Alice, Let's Eat.* New York: Random House, 1978.

Woolfolk, Margaret. *Cooking with Berries.* New York: Clarkson N. Potter, 1979.

The World Atlas of Food. New York: Simon & Schuster, 1974.

BASIC PIE PASTRY

2 cups presifted flour
1/2 teaspoon salt
1/2 cup (1 stick) chilled or frozen
butter or margarine, cut into
pieces

3 tablespoons vegetable
shortening
1/3 cup ice water

In a food processor, sift together flour and salt by pulsing on and off for several seconds. Add butter and shortening and process about 10 seconds until mixture resembles coarse meal.

With motor running, pour ice water through feed tube. Process 20 to 30 seconds or just until dough forms a ball (if you process it past this point, pastry will get overworked and tough). If dough doesn't form a ball, shape it with your hands. Dough is ready if it holds together when you pinch it with your fingers. Divide dough into 2 equal parts and wrap in wax paper or plastic wrap. Chill for 30 minutes.

Place 1 ball of dough on a lightly floured surface and flatten by tapping with a rolling pin into a thick disk. Dust top of dough with a little flour and rub some onto rolling pin. Roll out dough from the center outwards, lifting and turning dough every few strokes and adding flour sparingly as necessary. (Too much flour will toughen dough.) Roll into a circle about 2 inches larger in diameter than the top of the pie pan.

Fold dough gently into quarters, place in pie pan, and unfold it. Press lightly to fit contours of pan without stretching dough. Trim overhang, if necessary, to 1 inch and fold it under to form a thick edge. Flute by pinching in alternate directions with thumbs and forefingers or crimp with the tines of a fork, as desired. If recipe calls for unbaked pie shell, proceed with recipe at this point.

To partially prebake pie shell: Preheat oven to 425°F. Prick shell all over the bottom with the tines of a fork and chill again for 30 minutes. (This will relax the gluten, making pastry more tender, and reduce shrinkage.) Place on lower shelf of preheated oven for 15 minutes, until dough loses its translu-

cency but is not yet browned. Check it from time to time to pierce any air bubbles that may form. Remove from oven and cool on a wire rack before filling.

To fully prebake pie shell: Preheat oven to 425°F. Prick shell all over bottom with the tines of a fork and chill for 30 minutes. Place on lower shelf of preheated oven for 10 minutes, checking it from time to time to pierce any air bubbles that may form. Lower heat to 350°F. and bake for 10 to 15 minutes more, until pastry is golden brown. Remove from oven and cool on a wire rack before filling.

To make a double-crust pie: It is not necessary to flute or crimp bottom crust; just leave a 3/4 inch overhang. Roll out second ball of dough as directed above to a diameter 1 1/2 inches wider than the top of pie pan. Ease top crust over filled bottom crust and trim overhang to 3/4 inch. Fold top crust over the bottom around the edge and press to seal. Crimp or flute edges if desired. Make slits in top to let steam escape. Bake as directed in recipe.

YIELD: 2 9-INCH PIE SHELLS OR 1 DOUBLE-CRUST PIE

BASIC PIZZA DOUGH

Pizza dough is so quick to make in a food processor and so easy to roll out that you shouldn't feel intimidated. The only thing that's time-consuming is the hour and a half it takes to rise. To get the crispest possible crust, you will either have to bake the pizza directly on unglazed tiles in your oven, or buy a proper pizza pan, the best being those made of heavy black steel. You can also use a baking stone.

The possibilities for toppings are endless: smoked ham and multicolored peppers on a fresh tomato sauce base; Creamed Spinach (page 8) and mushrooms; pesto with eggplant and peppers (page 31) or with almost any leftover crisp-cooked vegetables; ratatouille—all crowned with cheese. Whatever your toppings, the process is more or less the same: Spread the unbaked crust lightly with a sauce, add the toppings, and sprinkle with cheese. Each pizza will take 1/2 pound grated mozzarella and 2 ounces grated Parmesan, mixed—or almost any combination of hard or semi-hard cheeses you wish.

1 package dry yeast
1 teaspoon sugar
2 cups presifted flour
1/2 teaspoon salt
2 tablespoons olive oil
cornmeal for pan

Stir yeast and sugar into 1/4 cup warm water. Let stand for 5 minutes to proof yeast; mixture should become frothy.

In a food processor, combine flour, salt, olive oil, 1/2 cup additional warm water and the yeast mixture. Process on and off for a few seconds until the dough forms an elastic ball. Remove dough, knead briefly for a few seconds to make sure it's evenly blended, and place it in a lightly oiled bowl. Turn dough around once to coat the entire surface with oil. Cover with a dish towel and place in a warm, draft-free place for 1½ hours to rise.

When dough has risen, preheat oven to 450°F. Punch down dough and roll out on a floured surface to a diameter several inches larger than your pan. Rotate the dough as you roll it out to make a perfect circle. Sprinkle pizza pan with a little cornmeal. Sprinkle a little flour over the top of the dough, fold in half and then in half again. Place this "wedge" on pizza pan and

unfold. Dough should overhang pan all around. Roll up the excess to form a rim around the edge. Brush dough with a little olive oil and add toppings.

Bake for 20 to 25 minutes until crust and cheeses are golden brown. Serve immediately.

YIELD: CRUST FOR 1 12-INCH PIZZA

SWEET SHORT TART SHELL

This recipe *could* be cut in half to make pastry for only 1 tart. But if you're going to the trouble, why not make the whole amount? The raw dough can be refrigerated for a few days—or frozen—until you're ready to make the second tart. This is a perfect recipe for anyone who is intimidated by rolling pins, since the dough is pressed by hand into the tart shell. It makes a crunchy, almost cookielike crust.

2¼ cups flour
1/2 cup sugar
2 tablespoon vanilla extract
2 egg yolks
2 sticks softened butter or
    margarine

Mix together flour, sugar, vanilla and egg yolks. Cut butter into small pieces and work it into the dough with your hands. Form into a ball, wrap in plastic wrap or wax paper, and refrigerate for an hour.

When dough has chilled, butter the bottom and sides of a 10-inch flan ring or fluted-edge tart pan (or 2). Sprinkle sugar over the surface and shake off the excess. Remove dough from refrigerator and cut ball in half. Cut slices about 1/8-inch thick from the dough and press into flan ring, using small pieces of dough to fill any cracks.

To prebake tart shell: Preheat oven to 400°F. Place a piece of aluminum foil under the flan ring to catch any leakage, and bake shell for 10 minutes. Remove from oven, prick bottom with a fork, lower temperature to 350°F. and bake for 6 to 7 minutes more, until golden. Remove from oven and cool in flan ring before filling.

YIELD: PASTRY FOR 2 10-INCH FLAN RINGS

FRESH TOMATO SAUCE

This sauce is equally good over pasta, pizza, veal or chicken. Since the job of peeling and seeding the tomatoes is fairly tedious, you might as well make a large amount of sauce. Just think of how good it will taste on a bleak day in February, when you haven't seen a fresh tomato in months. When you seed the tomatoes, do it over a strainer and bowl. The seeds will strain out and what's left is pure fresh tomato juice. Just add salt and pepper. (This juice can be frozen and used later in recipes such as Celery-Flavored Winter Tonic, page 70.)

7 pounds very ripe local tomatoes	1/4 cup chopped fresh basil
1/4 cup olive oil	1/4 cup chopped fresh parsley
1 large Spanish onion, chopped	2 tablespoons chopped fresh
2 cloves garlic, chopped	thyme, or 1½ teaspoons dried
2 stalks celery, chopped	2 bay leaves
2 large carrots, thinly sliced	freshly ground pepper to taste
2 teaspoons salt	
1 6-ounce can tomato paste	

Peel tomatoes by dipping them in boiling water for 10 seconds; their skins will then come off easily. Quarter each tomato and gently squeeze out the seeds and juice. Chop the pulp. You will have about 12 cups of pulp. Set aside.

In a large stockpot, heat the oil and sauté onion until just wilted. Add garlic, celery and carrots, and sauté for 5 minutes more.

Add tomatoes, tomato paste and bay leaves. Bring to a boil, then lower heat and simmer, uncovered, for 40 minutes, stirring occasionally. Add herbs and simmer 5 minutes more. Add salt and pepper. Remove from heat.

When sauce has cooled slightly, discard bay leaves and purée sauce in batches in a food processor until almost smooth (a little chunky texture makes it more interesting). Cool, then chill. Freeze in 3-cup batches.

YIELD: 9 TO 10 CUPS OF SAUCE

PESTO

This basil-flavored sauce of Genoese origin has become a virtual staple in American kitchens. It's most often used over pasta (the amount in the recipe below should be tossed quickly with 2 pounds of cooked, drained spaghetti or other pasta). It is equally good on potatoes, with many vegetables, on pizza, or spread in the cavity of a whole fish before grilling or baking. Pesto freezes well, indefinitely, but should be brought to room temperature before tossing with hot pasta.

3 cups fresh basil leaves, tightly packed	1/4 cup chopped fresh parsley
1 teaspoon salt	1/2 cup grated Parmesan cheese
1 clove garlic, cut in half	optional: 1/4 cup pignoli (pine nuts)
4 tablespoons (1/2 stick) butter or margarine	
1/4 cup olive oil	

Wash the basil and pull off the leaves, discarding any tough stems. Dry in a salad spinner.

Place all ingredients in a food processor and process, scraping down sides with a spatula if necessary, for 2 or 3 minutes until a thick purée is formed.

YIELD: 1 CUP

Break egg into container of electric blender or food processor. Add lemon juice, mustard, salt and pepper and blend at top speed until mixture is thick and foamy.

Uncover container and, continuing to blend at top speed, pour the oil very slowly, drop by drop, into the center of the egg mixture, until mayonnaise begins to thicken; then continue adding oil in a thin stream. If mixture gets too thick, you can add 1 tablespoon of warm water.

YIELD: 1 TO 1¼ CUPS

Garlic mayonnaise: Add 1 large clove garlic, cut in several pieces, to blender in first step of recipe.

CHICKEN OR TURKEY BROTH

If you freeze poultry parts to save up for making broth, take the time to strip off the skin and fat before you put them in the freezer. That way you can use them straight from the freezer, without thawing. Turkey bones, by the way, make a wonderfully full-bodied broth.

1 large onion
2 cloves garlic
2 carrots
2 stalks celery, with leaves
2 parsnips, if available
10 whole peppercorns

1 teaspoon dried thyme
2 bay leaves
several sprigs of parsley
4 pounds chicken or turkey bones, carcass, gizzards, et cetera

BASIC RECIPES

Peel vegetables, cut into chunks and place in the bottom of a large (8-quart) stockpot. Add peppercorns and herbs.

Trim any fat or skin off chicken parts, add to pot and pour in enough cold water to barely cover. Bring to a boil, then reduce heat so that bubbles just barely break the surface. Skim off any foam that rises to the surface. Simmer uncovered for 2½ hours.

Strain broth in a cheesecloth-lined strainer, pressing out all the juices. Let cool to room temperature, then refrigerate. If desired, freeze in 2-cup or 4-cup containers, depending upon your cooking needs. Before using, skim off fat. Salt as needed.

YIELD: ABOUT 3 QUARTS

HERB VINAIGRETTE

There are a thousand variations on the vinegar-and oil theme. Here is my favorite, along with some useful alternatives. You can vary the herbs according to whatever is in season or available in the market.

¼ cup balsamic vinegar
1 teaspoon dry mustard
salt and freshly ground pepper to taste
2 teaspoons finely chopped chives

2 teaspoons finely chopped parsley
1 teaspoon finely chopped tarragon or basil or marjoram or to taste
½ cup extra-virgin olive oil
¼ cup corn oil

In a 10-to12-ounce jar, place vinegar, mustard, salt, pepper and herbs. Cap the jar and shake well. Add oils and shake well again.

YIELD: 1 CUP

Creamy herb vinaigrette: Make recipe above in a food processor rather than by hand, adding oil slowly with motor running as you would for a mayonnaise.

Raspberry vinaigrette: Substitute ¼ cup raspberry vinegar.

Mustard vinaigrette: Substitute 1½ teaspoons Dijon mustard for the dry mustard.

Garlic vinaigrette: Add 1 clove garlic, crushed, before adding the oil.

MAYONNAISE

1 egg
juice of 1/2 lemon
1 teaspoon dried mustard
1/2 teaspoon salt

1/4 teaspoon white pepper
1 cup corn oil, or half corn oil and half olive oil

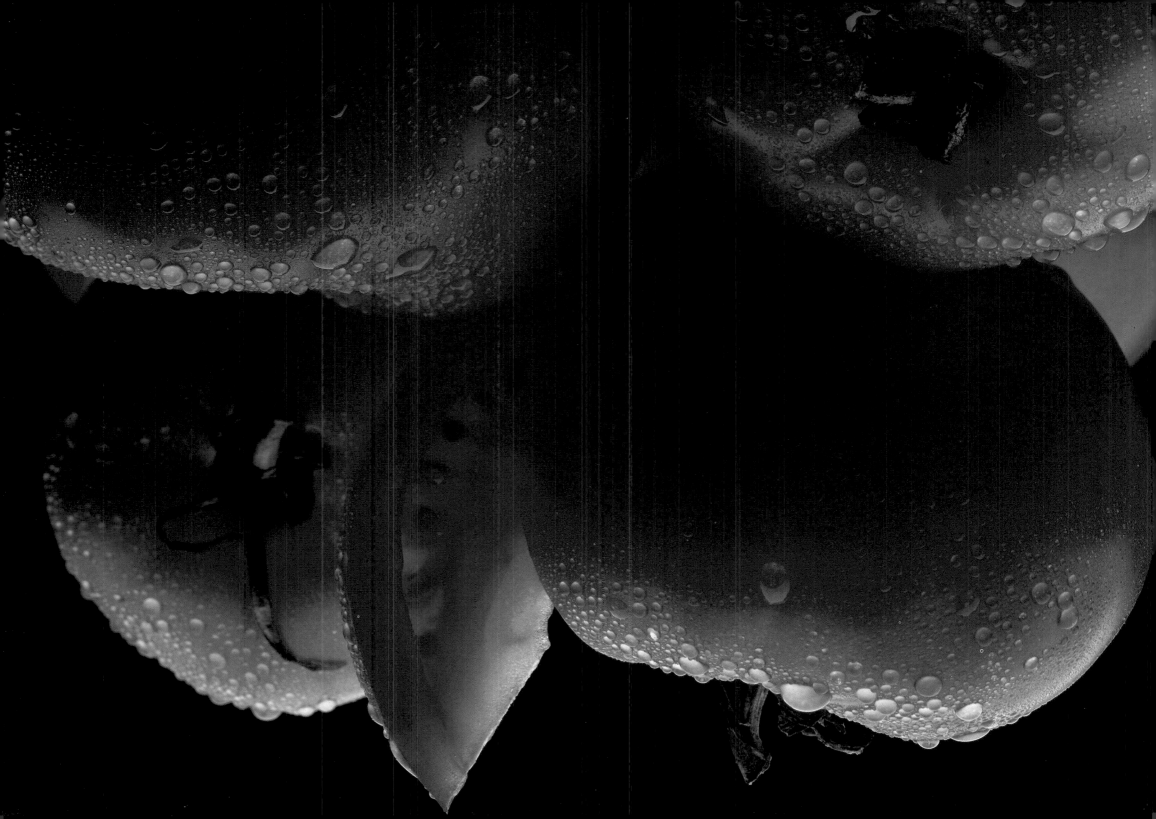

LIME CHEESECAKE

Everyone occasionally needs a binge and the tangy lime takes the edge off the richness in this satisfying cake. You'll need about three limes for this recipe—and the cake is best made the day before serving so it has time to chill.

1 cup graham cracker crumbs
1 1/4 cups sugar
4 tablespoons (1/2 stick) butter or margarine, melted
3 8-ounce packages cream cheese, softened
3 eggs

1/4 cup plus 1 tablespoon freshly squeezed lime juice
2 tablespoons grated lime rind
1 1/2 cups sour cream

Preheat oven to 250°F.

To make crust, combine crumbs, 2 tablespoons of the sugar and the melted butter. Press mixture into bottom and sides of an 8-inch springform pan. Bake 5 minutes. Remove from oven and cool.

Place 1 package of the cream cheese and 1 egg in a large mixer bowl, and beat thoroughly. Alternate remaining packages of cream cheese and eggs, beating well after each addition. Gradually add 1 cup of the sugar with 1/4 cup of the lime juice. Beat at medium speed for 10 minutes. Stir in lime rind. Pour into crust and bake 25 minutes. Turn off heat, let cake stay in oven 45 minutes more, then remove.

Now preheat oven to 350°.F.

Combine sour cream with remaining 2 tablespoons sugar and 1 tablespoon lime juice. Gently spread topping evenly over warm cake surface. Return cake to oven and bake 10 minutes. Cool on wire rack, then refrigerate for several hours or overnight before removing from springform.

YIELD: 10 TO 12 SERVINGS

LEMON CONSERVE

If you like the taste of lemon, you can't do much better than slathering this rich and tangy spread on a slice of toasted wheat bread. It is also delicious spread between the layers of a cake, or (sparingly) on the bottom of a fresh berry or banana tart. You'll need about three large lemons, more if they are small, to get one cup of juice.

6 egg yolks
1 1/2 cups sugar
2 tablespoons freshly grated lemon rind

1 cup fresh lemon juice
1/2 cup (1 stick) butter or margarine

In the top of a double boiler, mix egg yolks with sugar, lemon rind and lemon juice and cook, stirring, over boiling water until sugar dissolves.

Add butter and continue cooking for 15 to 20 minutes, stirring constantly, until mixture is smooth and very thick.

Cool, then chill. Mixture will thicken further as it cools.

YIELD: 2 1/2 CUPS

ARLINE YOUNGMAN'S GRAPEFRUIT SORBET

This is not as sweet as it sounds, since the sugar counteracts the tartness of the grapefruit, but you can use less sugar if you wish. It can be served with cassis or raspberry purée, although it's quite wonderful all by itself. You'll need about three medium grapefruits to get two cups of juice and pulp.

2 cups sugar	4 cups water
2 cups freshly squeezed	grapefruit juice, pulp included

Combine sugar and water. Bring to a boil and stir until all sugar is melted.

Add grapefruit juice and let cool. Chill thoroughly in refrigerator.

Pour into container of ice cream maker and freeze according to manufacturer's instructions.

YIELD: ABOUT 2 QUARTS

ORANGE-GLAZED PECAN CAKE

2 cups flour	1 cup sugar
1 teaspoon baking powder	3 eggs, separated
1 teaspoon baking soda	3/4 cup sour cream
4 ounces pecans, finely chopped	4 tablespoons freshly grated orange rind
1 cup (2 sticks) butter or margarine (about 1 cup)	generous pinch of salt

Glaze

3/4 cup sugar	4 tablespoons fresh orange juice

Preheat oven to 350°F.

Sift together flour, baking powder and baking soda. Combine with pecans.

In another bowl, cream butter and sugar and add egg yolks only, 1 at a time, beating well until each is incorporated.

Add the dry ingredients alternately with the sour cream. Stir in the orange rind.

In a separate bowl, beat the egg whites with the salt until they form peaks. Fold into batter. Butter and flour a 9-inch springform pan. Gently pour in batter. Bake for 1 hour or until a toothpick inserted in center comes out clean.

Just before removing cake from oven, make the glaze: Mix sugar and orange juice in a small pan and bring to a boil, stirring to dissolve sugar. When the cake is removed from the oven, prick the top all over with a paring knife. Brush the hot glaze gradually over the hot cake until all is absorbed. Cool cake in the pan.

YIELD: 10 TO 12 SERVINGS

LEMON POUND CAKE

"Pound cake" was so designated because its major ingredients—butter, sugar, eggs and flour—were originally measured by the pound. Today's recipes, mercifully, are more temperate, though still rich.

1 cup (2 sticks) butter or
  margarine
2½ cups sugar
6 extra-large eggs
3 cups flour
½ teaspoon salt
2 teaspoons baking powder

1 cup sour cream
grated rind of 2 lemons
2 teaspoons lemon extract

Glaze

juice of 1 lemon
½ cup sugar

Preheat oven to 350°F.

In an electric mixer, cream together butter and sugar until soft and fluffy. Add eggs one at a time, beating well after each addition.

In a separate bowl, sift together flour, salt and baking powder. Add alternately to batter with sour cream, beginning and ending with dry ingredients. Beat just until smooth after each addition, carefully incorporating all ingredients. Stir in lemon rind and extract—batter will be thick. Spoon into buttered and floured 10-inch tube pan.

Bake for 1¼ hours or until toothpick inserted in center comes out clean. But start testing at 1 hour since ovens can vary and cake should be moist, not overbaked.

Just before removing cake from oven, prepare glaze: Mix lemon juice and sugar in a small pot and bring to a boil to dissolve sugar. Place cake on a rack and let stand for 5 minutes. Prick the top of the cake with a paring knife, then brush the hot glaze over it until it is all absorbed. Let cake rest for an hour before removing it from the pan.

YIELD: 12 OR MORE SERVINGS

IVAN'S LEMON-LIME PIE

You'll need 2 to 3 lemons and 3 to 4 limes for this recipe depending on size, juiciness and your own diligence with the squeezer. This is a variation on key lime pie. Make it a day ahead or early in the day so it has time to chill.

2 9-inch partially prebaked pie
  shells made with Basic Pie
  Pastry (page 148)
2 14-ounce cans sweetened
  condensed milk
4 egg yolks
grated rind of one lemon
grated rind of one lime

½ cup freshly squeezed lemon
  juice
½ cup freshly squeezed lime juice
6 egg whites
6 tablespoons sugar
1 teaspoon lemon juice
1 teaspoon lime juice

Preheat oven to 350°F.

Mix condensed milk with egg yolks and grated rinds. Gradually stir in ½ cup each of lemon and lime juice. (Mixture will thicken considerably.) Divide between pie shells.

In a clean bowl, beat egg whites until frothy. Add sugar and teaspoons of juices, and beat until stiff. Top each pie with the meringue mixture, making sure it touches the rim of the crust all around so it doesn't shrink away during baking. Bake for about 15 minutes, or until lightly browned. Cool, then chill.

YIELD: 2 PIES, OR 12 SERVINGS

One of the most versatile playthings of the botanist is the tangerine. Crossed with an orange, it becomes a "tangor" or temple orange; with a grapefruit, a "tangelo"; with both a grapefruit and a Seville orange, an "ugli fruit." Mandarin oranges are a variety of tangerine with lighter skin and fewer seeds.

TANGERINE ANGEL FOOD CAKE

Tangerines give a slightly more subtle taste than oranges in this recipe, but the two can be used interchangeably. Use extra-large eggs for your egg whites or add the white of an extra egg if yours are smallish. Do not grease the pan or the cake won't rise.

1¼ cups cake flour	2 tablespoons tangerine rind
1½ teaspoons cream of tartar	2 tablespoons tangerine juice
¼ teaspoon salt	
1½ cups sugar, preferably superfine	
12 egg whites, at room temperature	

Icing

⅓ cup butter or margarine	1 tablespoon tangerine rind
1½ cups confectioners' sugar	3 tablespoons tangerine juice

Preheat oven to 325°F.

Sift cake flour 4 times with ½ cup of the superfine sugar.

Beat egg whites with cream of tartar and salt until soft moist peaks are formed. Add remaining superfine sugar, beating in a little at a time until whites are quite stiff. Then add 2 tablespoons each of the tangerine rind and of the juice and mix thoroughly but gently.

Fold flour-sugar mixture into egg whites in small batches, gently and only until no flour shows. Turn batter into an ungreased 10-inch tube pan.

Bake for 1 hour. Remove from oven and invert pan.

When cake has cooled, release it from pan and top with the following icing: Cream butter with confectioners' sugar, blending well. Add remaining tangerine rind and juice and beat until smooth. This icing will sparingly cover the top and only partly cover the sides of the cake. If you wish, you can decorate the cake with tangerine segments, white membranes removed.

YIELD: 10 TO 12 SERVINGS

CHERYL MERSER'S PASTA WITH VODKA, LEMON AND SMOKED SALMON

This is a surprising and delicious blend of ingredients. The recipe also happens to be extremely quick and easy to prepare.

4 ounces smoked salmon	1 heaping teaspoon lemon peel
2 tablespoons chopped fresh chives	¾ cup heavy cream
2 tablespoons chopped fresh parsley	freshly ground pepper to taste
1 tablespoon butter or margarine	½ pound linguini
1 tablespoon minced shallots	½ pound green (spinach) linguini
½ cup vodka	optional: 2 ounces salmon eggs (for garnish)
juice of ½ lemon	

Boil water for pasta. Cut smoked salmon into bits and prepare herbs. Set aside.

In a large frying pan, melt butter and sauté shallots until wilted. Add vodka, lemon juice and lemon peel, and simmer until alcohol boils off and sauce is reduced a bit. Add cream and black pepper and simmer for a few minutes more.

Cook linguini according to package directions; drain and place in a warmed serving bowl. Add smoked salmon, herbs and sauce and toss quickly to blend. Garnish with salmon eggs.

YIELD: 4 SERVINGS

ORANGE-CURRIED CHICKEN

Any of the usual curry accompaniments—coconut, peanuts, additional chutney, raisins, et cetera—make a nice garnish for this dish.

7½ pounds of chicken parts	2 tablespoons flour
salt and freshly ground pepper to taste	1 cup freshly squeezed orange juice
¼ cup oil	1½ cups Chicken Broth (page 145)
2 tart apples, chopped	1 tablespoon grated orange rind
2 ribs celery, chopped	⅔ cup chopped mango chutney
2 onions, chopped	2 bay leaves
2 carrots, chopped	1 large or 2 small navel oranges, sectioned
3 to 4 tablespoons curry powder (or to taste)	

Season chicken pieces with salt and pepper. Heat oil in a large skillet and, in several batches, brown chicken on all sides. Add more oil if necessary. Remove chicken and keep warm in a large casserole.

Add apples, celery, onions and carrots to remaining oil in skillet and cook, stirring, until onion is translucent. Sprinkle with curry powder and flour and cook for about 1 minute longer. Gradually stir in orange juice, chicken broth, rind, chutney and bay leaves. Season with additional salt and pepper to taste. Bring to a boil and pour over chicken in casserole. Cover and simmer 30 minutes or until chicken is tender.

Just before serving, remove bay leaves, stir in orange segments and heat until just warmed through.

YIELD: 8 to 10 SERVINGS

LEMON-HERB SHISHKABOB

You can thread vegetables such as cherry tomatoes, onion chunks and eggplant cubes on the skewers with the lamb. Brush them liberally with leftover marinade.

1 teaspoon freshly grated lemon rind	½ teaspoon oregano
¼ cup freshly squeezed lemon juice	1 large onion, sliced
½ cup olive oil	3 large cloves garlic, mashed
1 teaspoon salt	2 tablespoons finely chopped parsley
freshly ground pepper to taste	2 pounds lamb or beef, cut in 2-inch cubes

Whisk together lemon rind and juice, oil, salt, pepper and oregano. Add onion, garlic and parsley, mixing well.

Toss lamb or beef in marinade and let stand in the refrigerator 6 to 10 hours.

Thread cubes on skewers when ready to cook. Grill over hot coals, turning once, until cubes are charred on both sides and yet still pink in the middle. Or if cooking indoors, rest skewers in a greased broiler pan. Place 3 inches from flame, and broil for about 10 minutes on each side.

YIELD: 6 TO 8 SERVINGS

AVGOLEMONO SOUP

This Greek soup was very popular about twenty years ago and hasn't been seen much since. The Greeks usually make it with rice, but by substituting orzo—tiny rice-shaped bits of pasta—and adding cubed cooked chicken, you create a substantial meal-opener or lunch dish for a cold winter day. This soup is also lovely in the summer, without the chicken, chilled and garnished with thin slices of lemon.

6 cups Chicken Broth (page 145)
1/2 cup orzo
1 teaspoon salt
3 eggs
1/4 cup fresh lemon juice
1 cup cubed cooked chicken
freshly snipped parsley to taste

In a large saucepan, bring broth, orzo and salt to a boil and simmer, covered, for 10 minutes until orzo is just tender. Remove from heat.

Beat the eggs vigorously until they are foamy and pale yellow, then beat in the lemon juice. Take about 2 cups of the hot broth and whisk it *slowly* into the egg mixture so eggs will not curdle. Pour back into saucepan and whisk well until soup thickens a bit.

Add chicken and stir until heated through. Place a sprinkling of parsley in each soup bowl and ladle in the soup.

YIELD: 6 AMPLE SERVINGS

ERIC'S TADPOLES
(ORANGE-CINNAMON DOUGHNUT PUFFS)

We call these "tadpoles" because the dough always seems to leave a little tail when you drop it into the hot oil. This recipe is fun to make with a child—but use caution: The fat can splatter so keep the child—and yourself—a safe distance away from the stove.

1 egg
1/4 cup sugar
1 cup flour
1/4 teaspoon salt
1 teaspoon baking powder
1/4 teaspoon ground cinnamon

1/2 cup freshly squeezed orange juice
1/2 cup milk
1/2 teaspoon grated orange rind
corn oil for frying
1/4 teaspoon cinnamon sugar

Mix egg and sugar together by hand. Combine flour, salt, baking powder and cinnamon in a separate bowl and add to egg mixture alternately with juice and milk. Stir in orange rind.

In a deep fryer or a deep, heavy saucepan, heat 2 to 3 inches of corn oil to 375°F. Drop in dough by teaspoon measures, 4 or 5 pieces at a time. Fry until golden brown, turning once to make sure the puffs brown evenly. Drain on paper towels.

Make cinnamon sugar by mixing 1 part cinnamon to 3 parts sugar. While doughnut puffs are still warm, roll them in the cinnamon sugar.

YIELD: ABOUT 3 DOZEN "TADPOLES"

In the citrus family, it all began about twenty million years ago with a thick-skinned large berry. Native to China, the first oranges were the kind we use for marmalade today, bitter and not much larger than big marbles. Arabs carried them to ancient Rome, but they disappeared with the end of the empire and weren't heard of in Europe again until the Moors brought them to Spain after their conquest. The Portuguese imported sweet oranges from Asia to Europe in the sixteenth century.

From the beginning, oranges were a symbol of wealth and exotic tastes. Orange flowers were used to scent baths and cosmetics and the fruit inspired the five golden balls on the Medici coat of arms. Among the kings of Europe, there was a rush to build opulent or-

ORANGES, GRAPEFRUIT, LEMONS, LIMES & TANGERINES

angeries to protect these tender plants. Oranges and other citrus fruits were unknown in the Americas until Columbus brought seedlings here on his second voyage, but the United States is now the world's largest producer of oranges.

"A grapefruit is a lemon that had a chance and took advantage of it," goes an anonymous saying, yet the grapefruit's citrus ancestor is not the lemon but something called a shaddock, the largest of the citrus fruits, sometimes weighing over 20 pounds. The shaddock originated in Asia and grows in the West Indies, where the mutation that produced the grapefruit probably occurred.

The citron, a bumpy lemon look-alike that is used only for its peel, is the ancestor of both lemons and limes, whose names derive from the Arab word *limah*. Lemons and limes are fussier than the orange. The lime is especially sensitive to frost, and the lemon languishes in very hot climates. They both contain a high percentage of citric acid. Sprinkle their juice over sliced apples, bananas, or any fruit that otherwise would turn brown when exposed to air.

The lime has performed some curious functions beyond garnishing summer drinks. Malaysian sorcerers jab it with pins to transmit the arrows of love to a sweetheart. British sailors were once required to drink its juice on long sea voyages (not such a hardship, considering that it was mixed with rum) to prevent scurvy, and were thereafter dubbed "limeys." New Caledonians rub it into their scalps to ward off lice. And it is reputed to remove rust spots from clothing.

Among the loose-skinned citruses are the tangerine, the mandarin orange, clementines and the ugli, which elevates the merely loose-skinned to the truly baggy. In general, these varieties are more perishable than the tight-skinned citrus fruits—on the other hand, they're a lot easier to peel. The origin of the tangerine is lost in history, but it got its name from Tangiers. The clementine was developed by a French missionary, Father Clement, in Algiers in 1902.

When you shop for any member of the citrus family, look for smooth skins, free of blemishes and soft spots, and fruit that feels heavy for its size. Tight-skinned varieties should be firm; loose-skinned ones can be puffy as long as they aren't bruised. Remember that fruit yields the most juice at room temperature.

SLICED KIWI AND BANANA WITH STRAWBERRY PURÉE

They say that kiwi tastes like a cross between strawberry and banana, and here's your chance to test the hypothesis. This is surely the dessert of ultimate virtue: beautiful to behold, and low in calories.

1 pint strawberries, hulled	*1 tablespoon cornstarch*
juice of 1/2 lemon	*6 kiwis*
1/2 cup sugar	*3 large bananas*

Place strawberries in blender with lemon juice and 1/4 cup water; purée until smooth. Press through a fine strainer into a medium-sized saucepan (sauce will foam up as it cooks so you'll need the extra space).

Add sugar to the puréed strawberries and bring to a boil. Lower heat and simmer for 5 minutes. Mix cornstarch with 1 tablespoon water and stir into purée. Stir for a minute or 2 until mixture thickens. Remove from heat, cool and chill.

Just before serving, peel kiwis and bananas. Place several tablespoons of strawberry purée in one corner of each dessert plate. Slice 1 kiwi and 1/2 banana into overlapping semi-circles around each pool of sauce. If you have any purée left over, it's delicious on ice cream.

YIELD: 6 SERVINGS (ABOUT 1 1/2 CUPS OF PURÉE)

PINEAPPLE CHAMPAGNE

Does it go without saying that you wouldn't use the best imported champagne for this festive drink? Use a 2 1/2-quart pitcher or punch bowl and chill it thoroughly.

2 ripe pineapples	*fresh strawberries with leaves*
1 bottle champagne, chilled	*intact*

Slice off leaves and bottom of pineapple and cut into lengthwise quarters. Remove core from each quarter and separate fruit from rind, cutting out "eyes" and any imperfections. Chop.

Purée in several batches in blender until completely liquefied, then press through a fine strainer to eliminate fibers. Chill well, putting in freezer for a short time if necessary.

When ready to serve, pour pineapple juice into chilled pitcher or bowl, add champagne and stir to mix well. Serve in chilled champagne glasses with a strawberry in each.

YIELD: 10 SERVINGS

The uninviting hairy brown skin of the kiwi fruit shouldn't deter you from delving further into its glorious green interior. Among its virtues are its high vitamin C content, its low calorie count (thirty per average-sized fruit) and the fact that it can be refrigerated for up to six months without any loss of flavor or texture.

FRESH PINEAPPLE TART WITH GINGERED WHIPPED CREAM

1 10-inch prebaked Sweet Short Tart Shell (page 147)
1 cup heavy cream
1 tablespoon superfine sugar
1 ripe pineapple
1 teaspoon ground ginger

Slice off leaves and bottom of pineapple and cut into lengthwise quarters. Remove core from each quarter and separate fruit from rind, cutting out "eyes" and any imperfections. Slice into 1/4-inch slices, and drain on paper towels.

Beat cream until thickened but not stiff. Mix sugar and ginger in a small cup, then stir in a few tablespoons of cream until well blended. Add to bowl and continue beating until cream forms soft peaks.

Distribute pineapple slices evenly on prebaked tart shell. Pile gingered whipped cream on top, and sprinkle with additional ginger. Chill until ready to serve, but no more than a few hours.

YIELD: 8 SERVINGS

KIWI CRISP

1/2 cup flour
1/2 cup granulated sugar
1/2 cup firmly packed brown sugar
pinch of salt
1/2 cup (1 stick) butter or margarine
1/4 cup tapioca beads
1 teaspoon grated lime rind
10 kiwi fruit
vanilla ice cream

Work together flour, brown sugar and butter to form a crumbly topping; chill.

Preheat oven to 450°F.

Peel and slice kiwi fruit—you should have about 4 cups.

Mix together granulated sugar, salt, tapioca and lime rind and toss gently with kiwi slices. Pour into a 9-inch ovenproof dish and cover with chilled topping.

Bake for 10 minutes, then reduce heat to 350°F. and bake 15 to 20 minutes longer, or until topping is golden brown. Serve warm with ice cream.

YIELD: 6 to 8 SERVINGS

CURRIED CHICKEN WITH PAPAYA

Unless you have a very large pan, fry the chicken in a few batches. If you crowd the pan, the chicken won't brown.

4½ pounds chicken parts
¼ cup flour
1 tablespoon curry powder
salt and freshly ground pepper to taste
4 tablespoons (½ stick) butter or margarine

1 cup chopped onion
1 tablespoon flour
1 teaspoon curry powder
2 cups Chicken Broth (page 145)
½ cup yogurt
1 papaya

Remove skin and fat from chicken parts and pat dry. Into a plastic bag pour flour, curry powder, salt and pepper. Shake chicken parts in bag, a few at a time, to coat with mixture. Shake off excess flour.

Melt 2 tablespoons of the butter in a large skillet or electric frying pan and sauté chicken until brown on all sides. Remove from pan.

Add remaining butter to pan and sauté onion until translucent. Add 1 tablespoon flour and curry powder and cook over low flame for 2 minutes, then add broth and stir until mixture reaches boiling point and thickens. Return chicken to pan, cover and simmer for 40 minutes. Let cool and skim off fat.

Remove chicken from pan. Blend yogurt into broth and heat just to boiling point.

Cut papaya in half lengthwise, pare skin and scoop out seeds. Slice both halves crosswise into 1/4-inch slices and add to pan with chicken, cooking only until papaya is heated through.

YIELD: 6 SERVINGS

BASHKA'S BANANA CHARLOTTE

You can use a ring mold or any wide 6-cup bowl or mold for this old-fashioned dessert. Just adjust the lady fingers and orange slices accordingly.

4 to 5 ripe bananas
juice of ½ lemon
½ cup freshly squeezed orange juice (including pulp)
1 tablespoon (1 package) gelatin
½ cup sugar

1 cup heavy cream
2 tablespoons sherry
1 teaspoon vanilla
4 or more ladyfingers, split
2 to 3 seedless oranges

Mash bananas in a large bowl or electric mixer. Add lemon juice and orange juice and beat until smooth.

Sprinkle gelatin over ¼ cup water and stir until dissolved.

Combine sugar and ¼ cup water in a small, heavy saucepan and heat until boiling point is reached and sugar dissolves. Remove from heat, add gelatin mixture and stir until that too is dissolved. Add to banana mixture and cool.

Whip the cream and fold into the cooled banana mixture. Add sherry and vanilla and reserve.

Oil a 6-cup ring mold and arrange ladyfingers in the bottom. Peel and slice oranges. Arrange them like wheels around outer circumference of the ring mold. Gently pour in banana mixture. Chill until firm. Unmold to serve.

YIELD: 8 SERVINGS

INDONESIAN COCONUT SOUP

This is a sweet soup that goes very well with spicy Indian or Indonesian appetizers. You will find the coconut cream, in cans, in most specialty food stores.

1 coconut	1 tablespoon shelled pistachio
4 cups milk	nuts, coarsely chopped
1/3 cup coconut cream	

Preheat oven to 450°F.

With a screwdriver and a hammer, pierce holes in 2 of the 3 eyes of the coconut. Pour off and discard the liquid.

Bake the coconut for 15 minutes, then put it on a hard surface and hit it all over with a hammer. The hard shell will fall away. Use a knife to pry off any remaining pieces.

With a vegetable parer, scrape off the brown inner skin and rinse the coconut meat to remove any brown specks; dry. Grate finely in a food processor or meat grinder.

Scald milk and pour over grated coconut. Steep for 20 minutes. Strain, reserving the milk.

Measure 1 cup of grated coconut and put back into coconut milk. Add coconut cream and mix well.

When ready to serve, heat until steaming and garnish with pistachio nuts.

YIELD: 6 SERVINGS

SENEGALESE SOUP

This soup is so good that you may want to make enough for a good-sized dinner party: on the other hand, you can easily cut the ingredients in half for a smaller group. This recipe is for a chilled soup but it can also be served hot.

4 tablespoons (1/2 stick) butter or margarine	2 green apples, peeled, cored and chopped
1 large Spanish onion, chopped	2 bananas, sliced
3 stalks celery, chopped	1/2 teaspoon Tabasco sauce
2 cloves garlic, crushed	2 teaspoons salt
2 tablespoons curry powder	freshly ground pepper to taste
7 cups Chicken Broth (page 145)	2 cups light cream
2 medium-sized ripe tomatoes, chopped	optional: 1 cup diced chicken and/or chopped watercress as a
2 medium potatoes, peeled and cubed	garnish

In a large stockpot, melt butter. Add onion, celery and garlic and cook until wilted. Add curry powder and stir until blended. Add chicken broth, tomatoes, potatoes, green apples and bananas and bring to a boil. Add Tabasco, salt and pepper, and simmer, covered, for 20 minutes or until solids are soft.

Purée mixture in several batches in a blender or food processor and chill. When ready to serve, stir in cream and correct seasonings. Add garnishes if desired.

YIELD: 10 TO 12 SERVINGS